The highest condition of art is artlessness.

Truth is always paradoxical.

He will get to the goal first who stands stillest.

There is one let better than any help, and that is, — *Let-alone.*

By sufferance you may escape suffering.

He who resists not at all will never surrender.

When a dog runs at you, whistle for him.

Say, Not so, and you will outcircle the philosophers.

Stand outside the wall, and no harm can reach you. The danger is that you be walled in with it.

For an impenetrable shield, stand inside yourself.

June 26, 1840 — Henry D. Thoreau

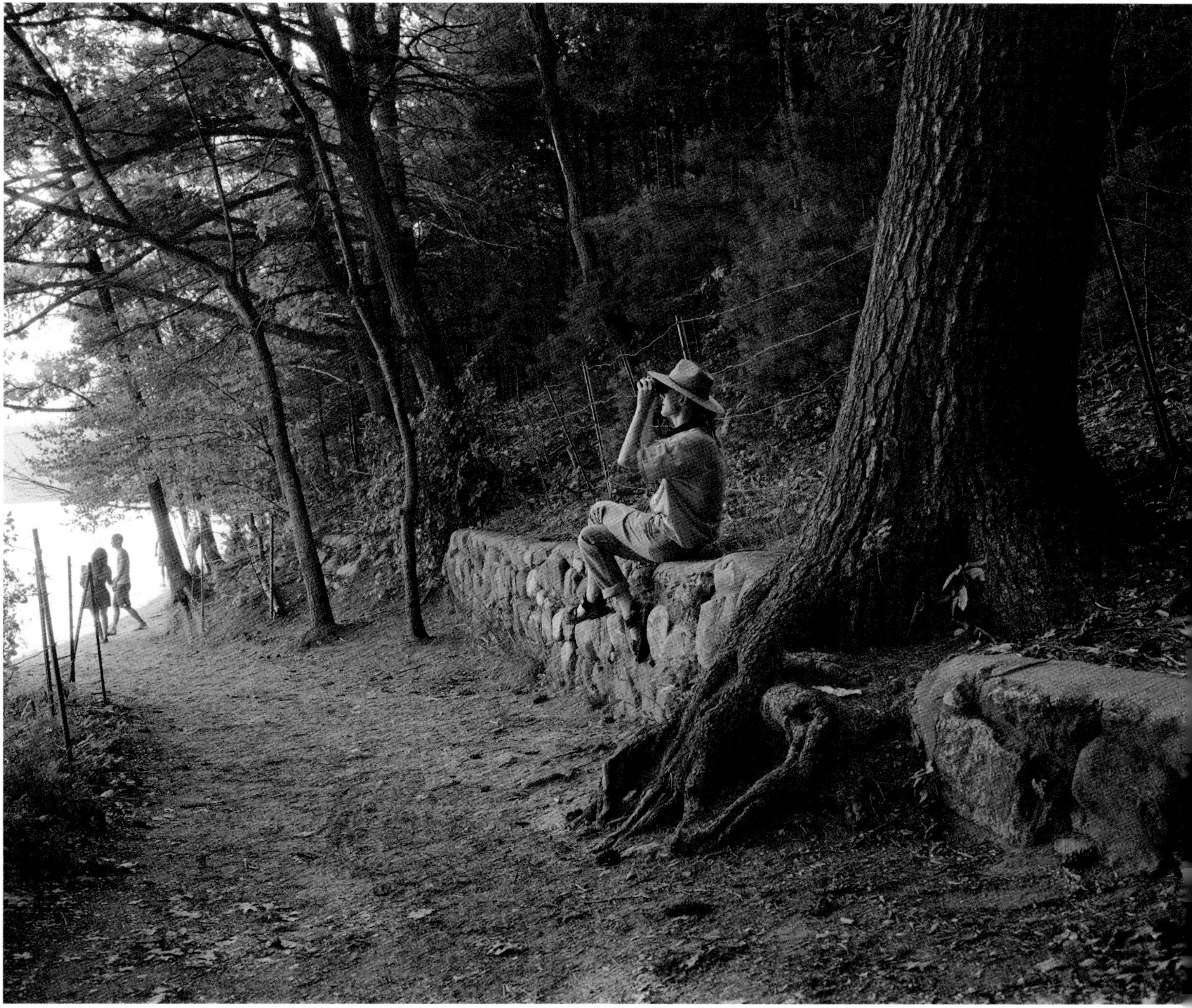

WALDEN

KEHRER

Photographs by S.B. WALKER

with an essay by Alan Trachtenberg

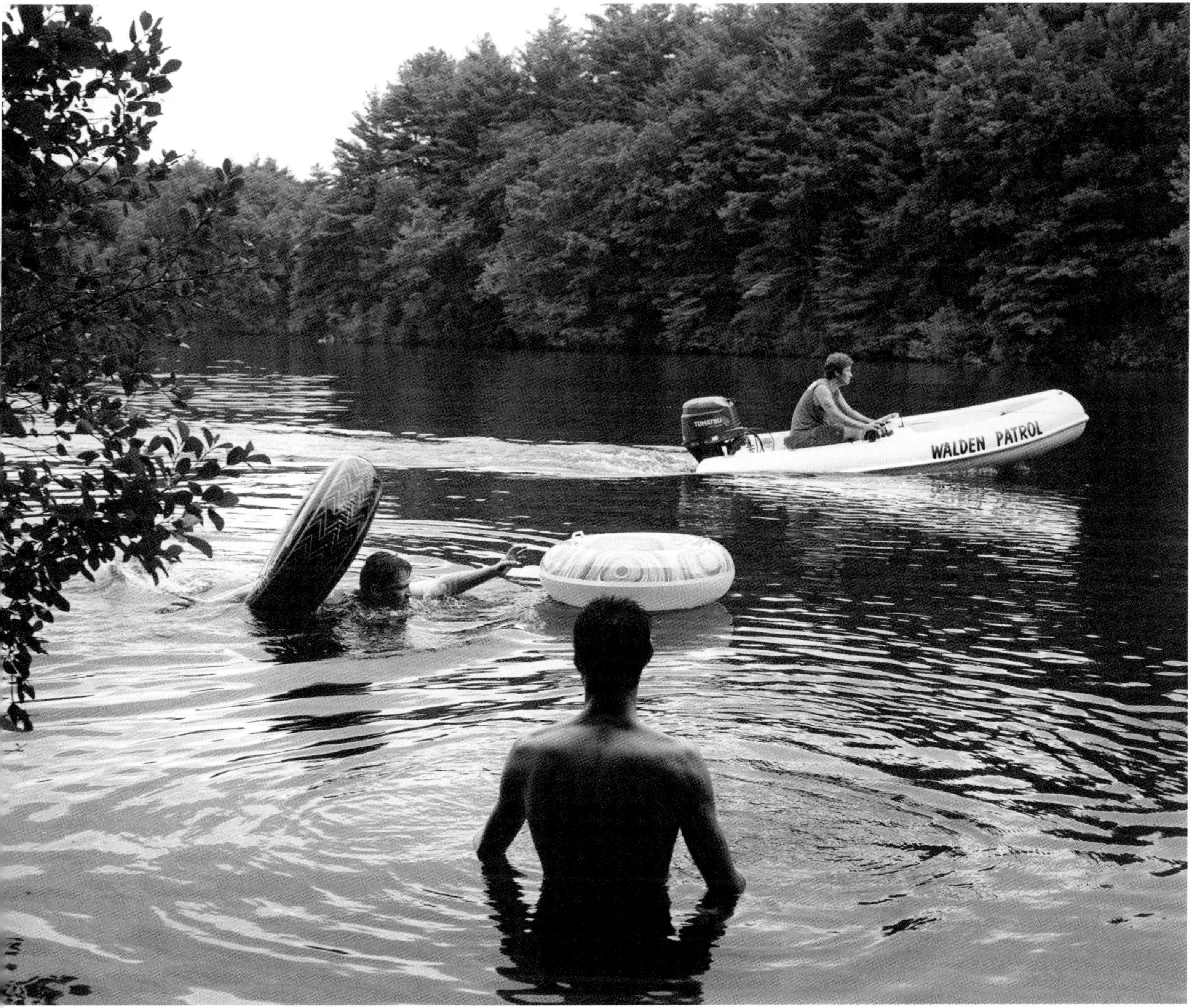
TOHATSU
WALDEN PATROL

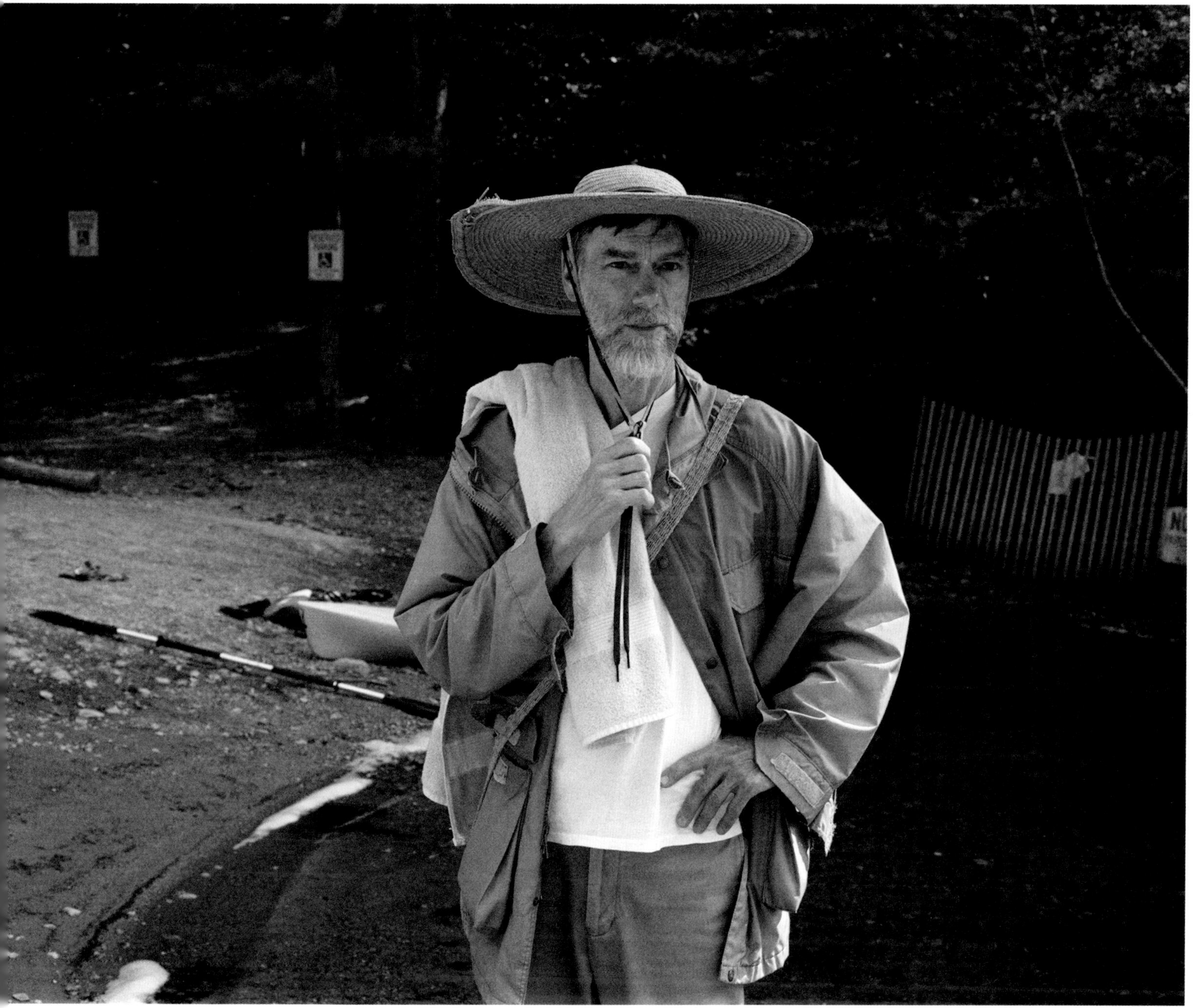

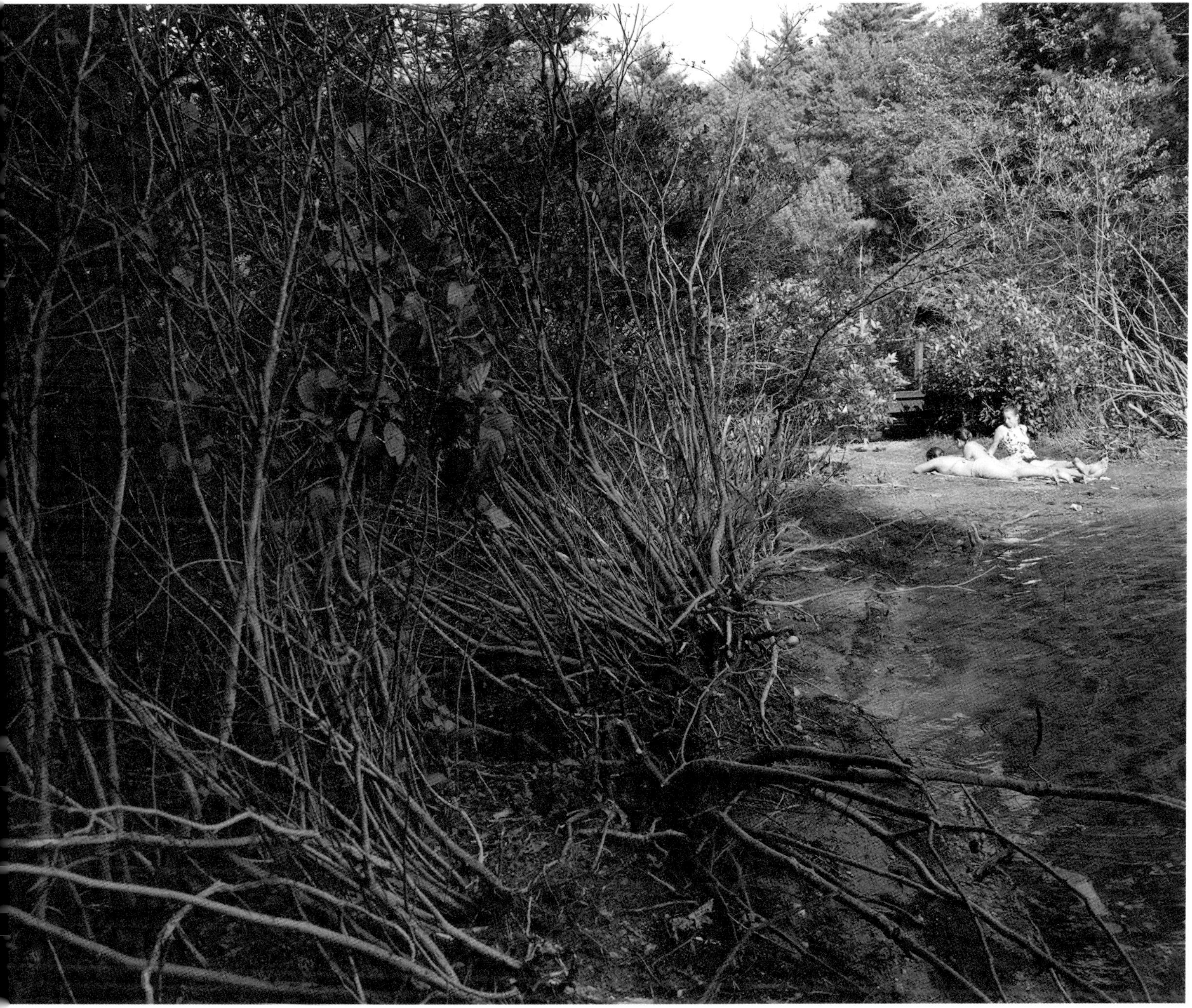

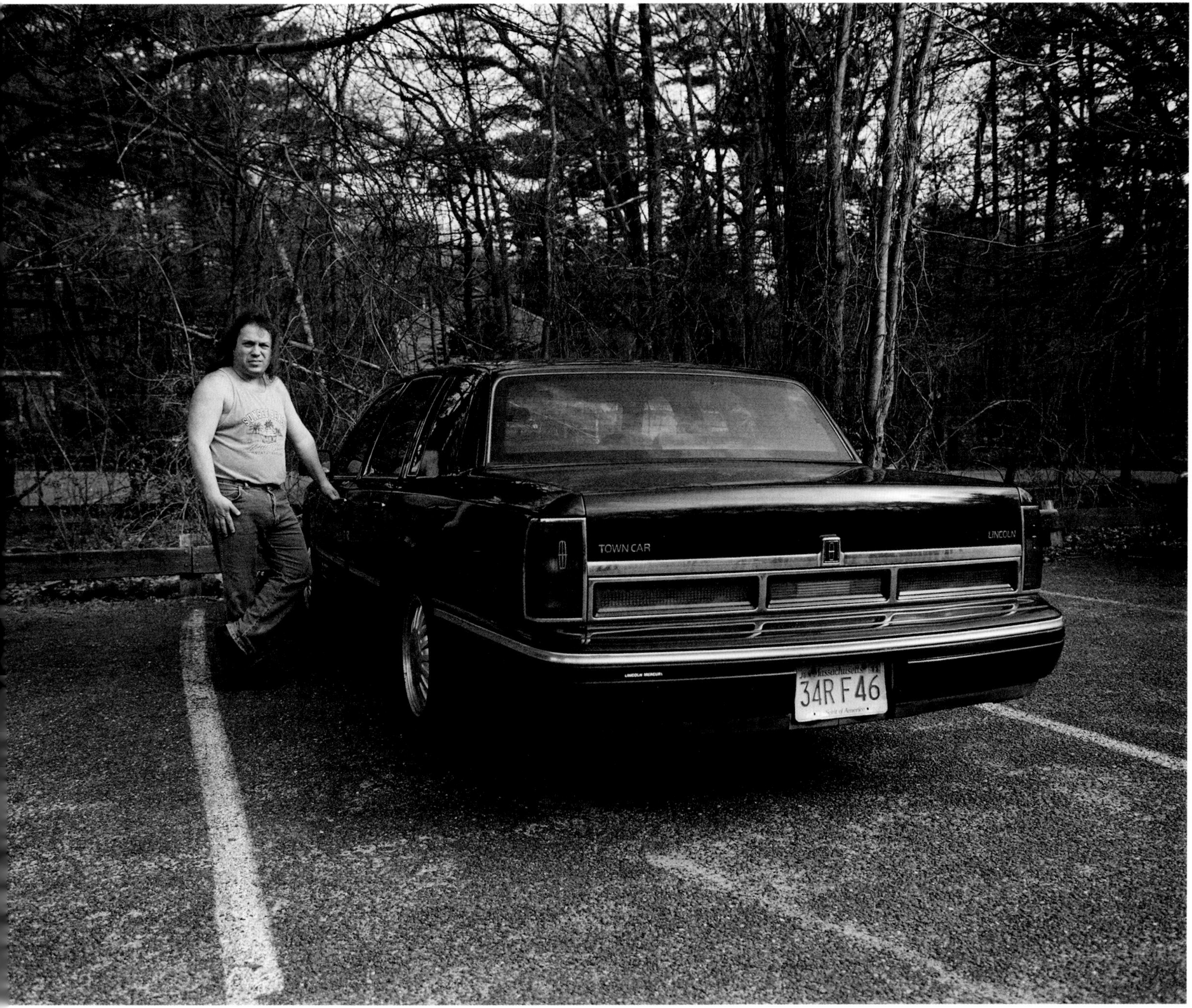
TOWN CAR
LINCOLN
34R F46

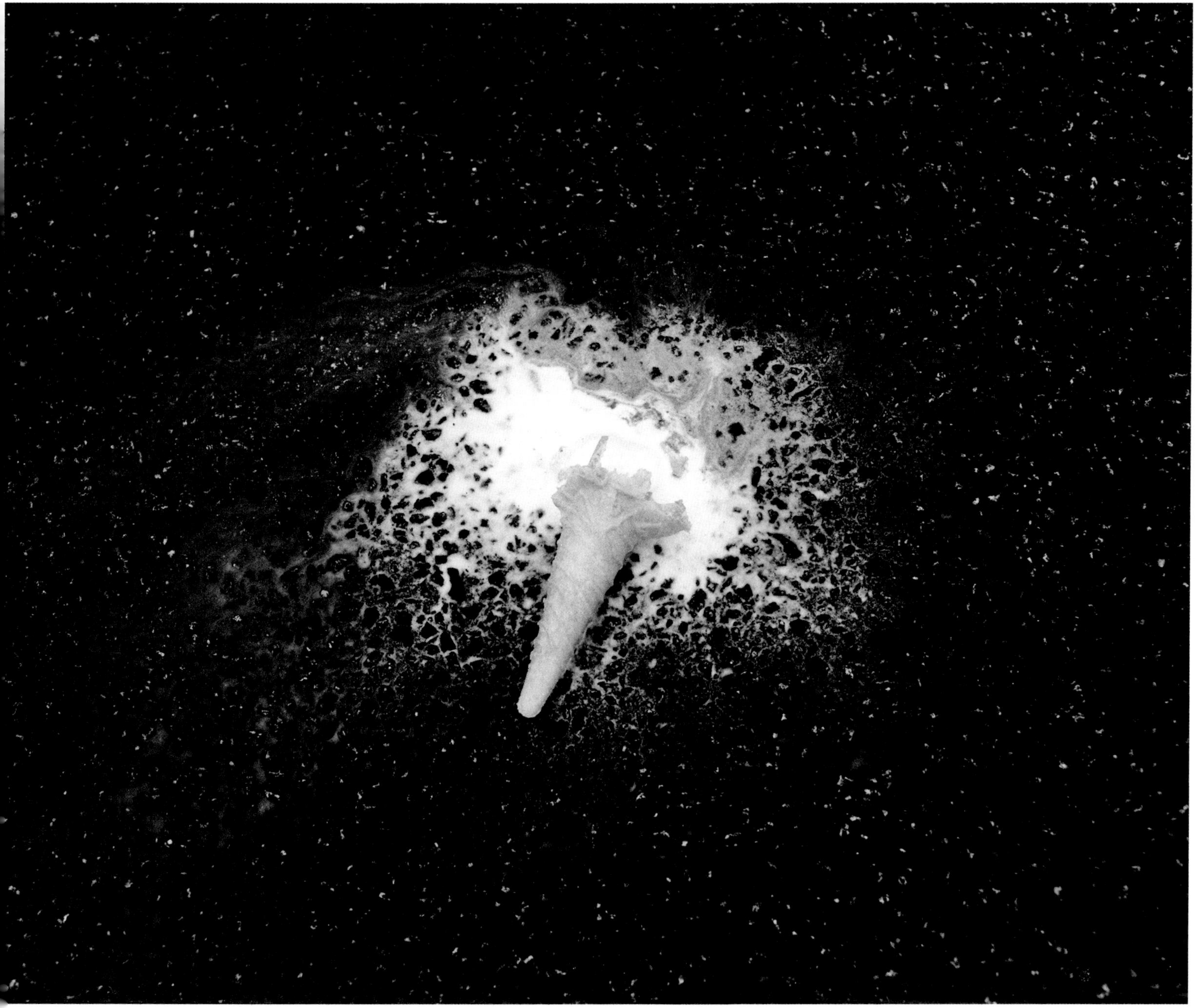

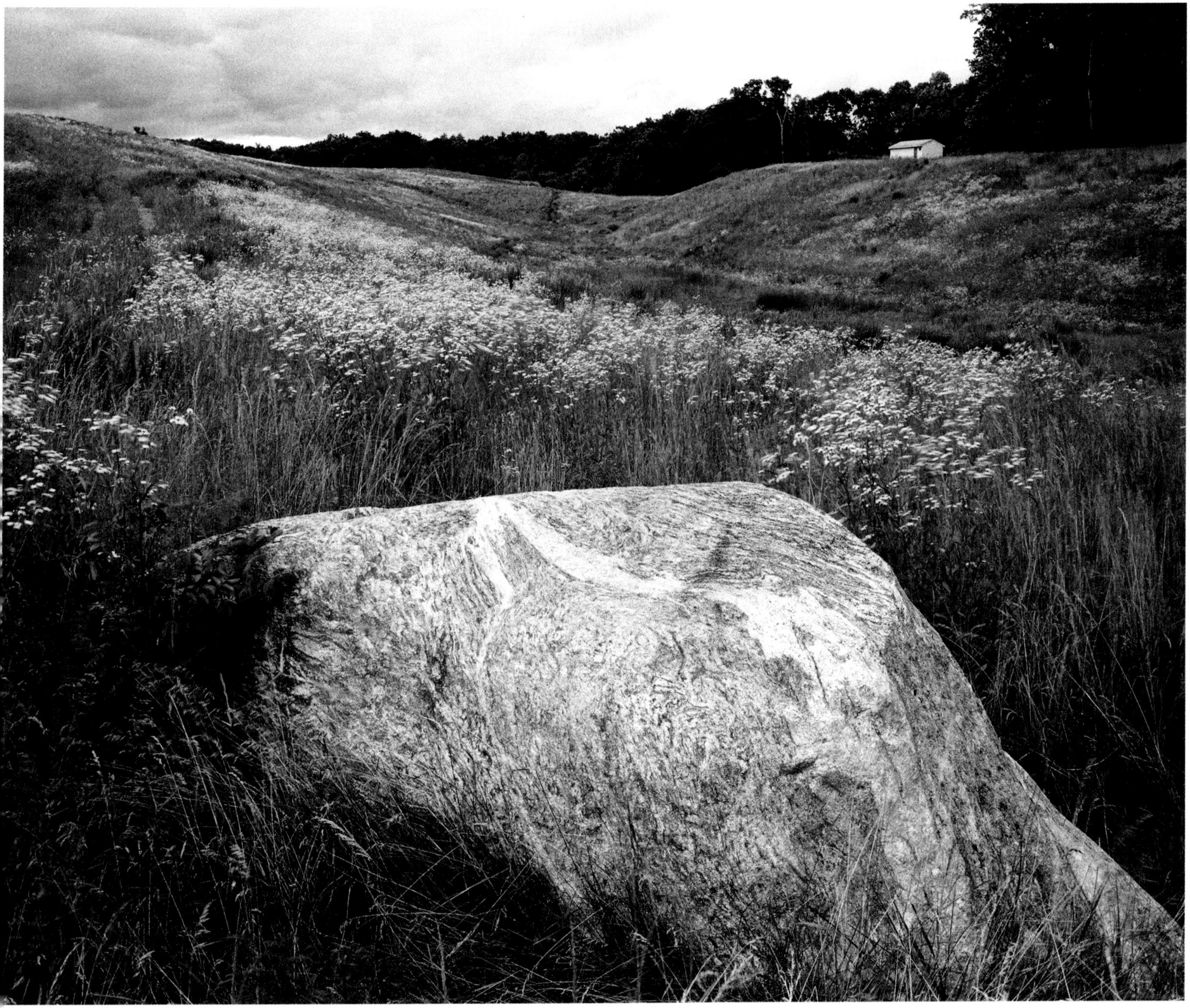

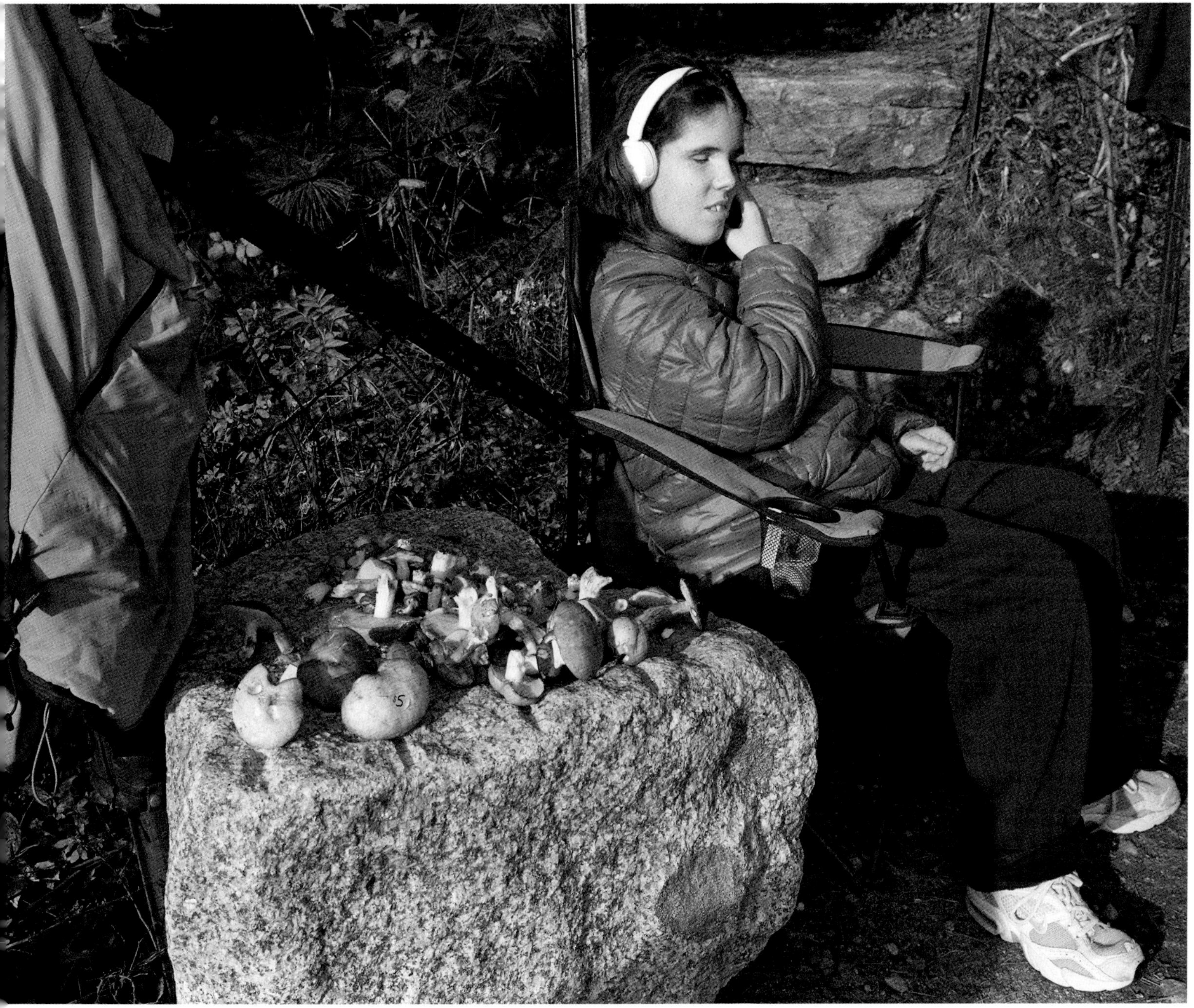

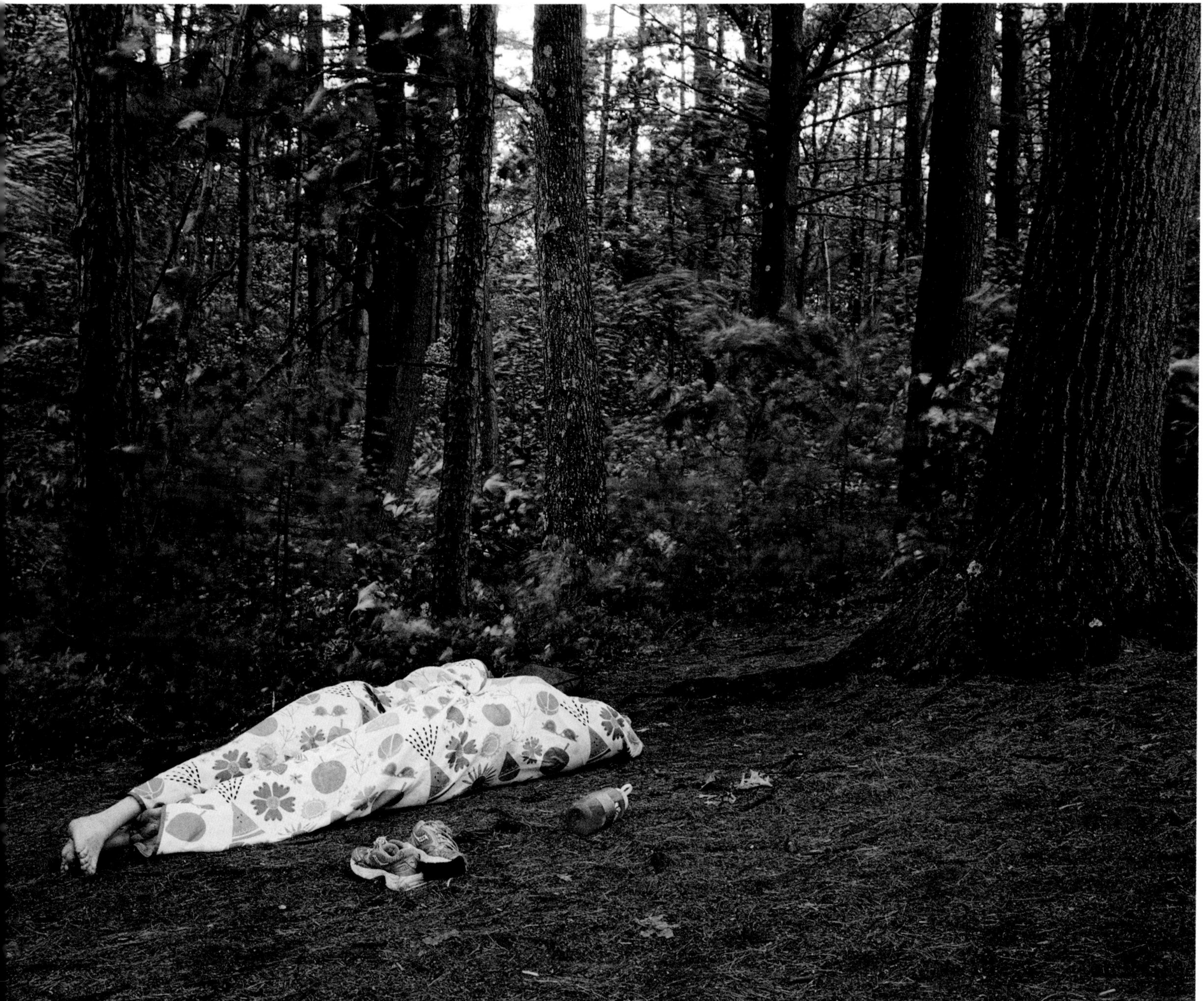

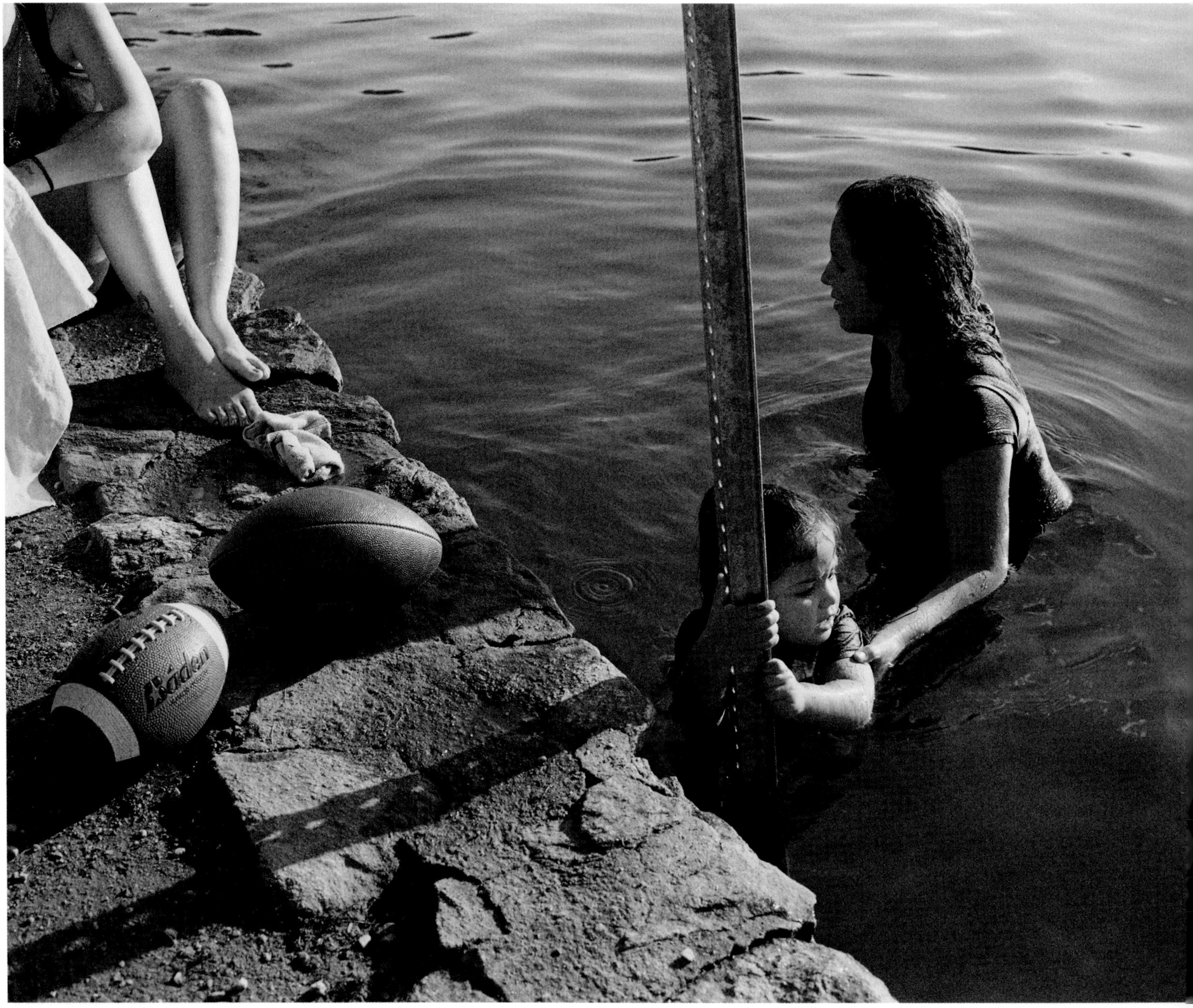
Baden

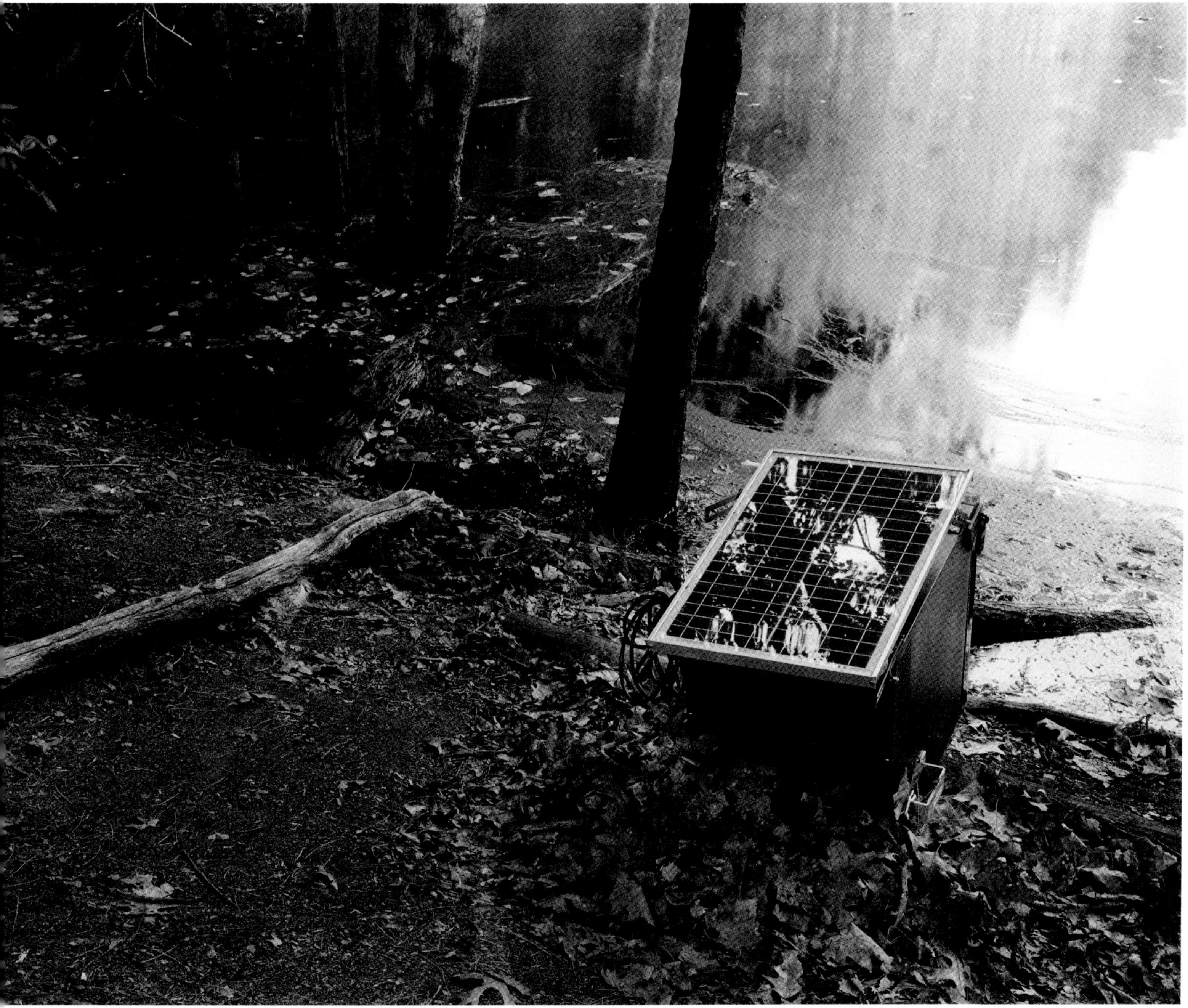

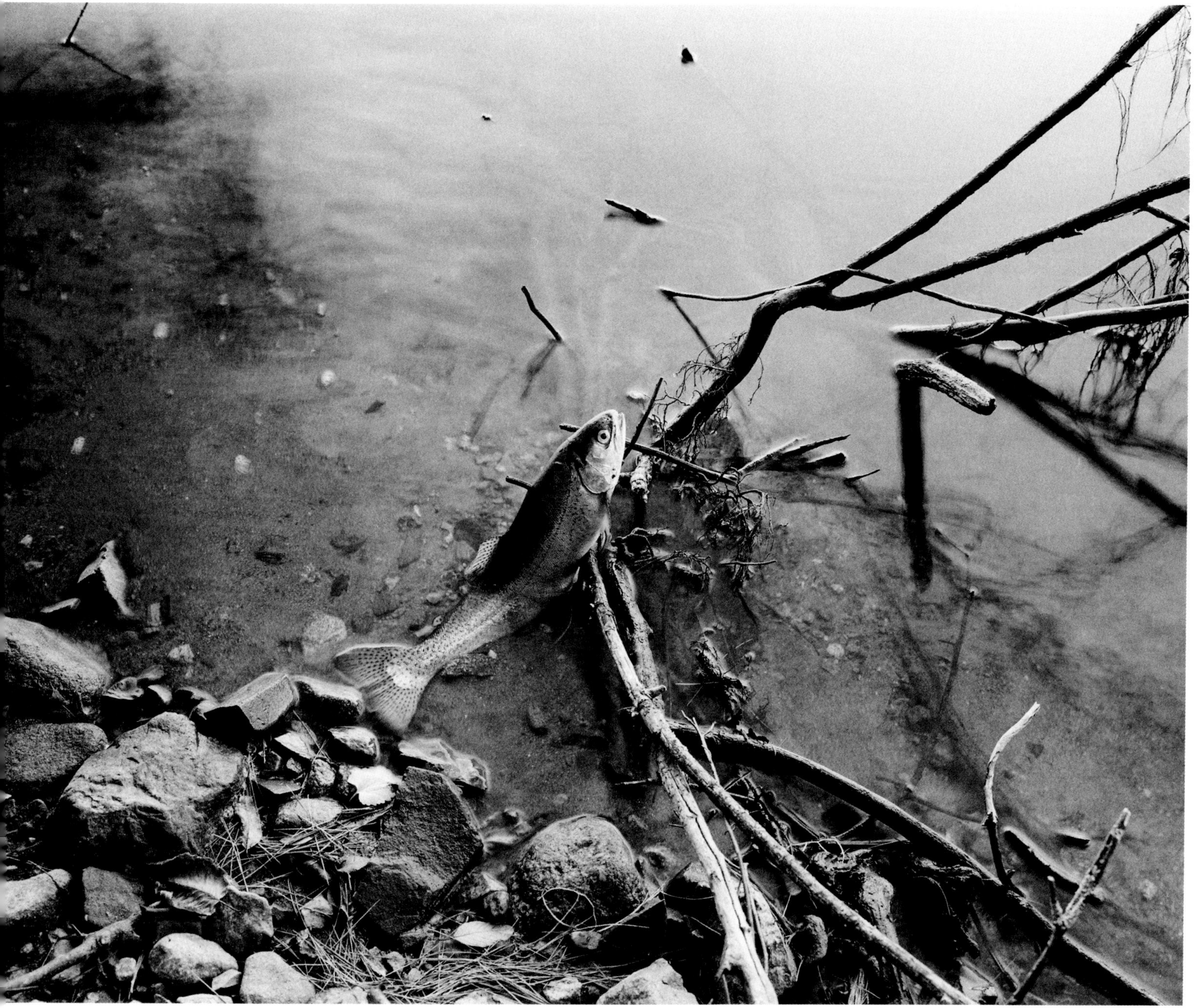

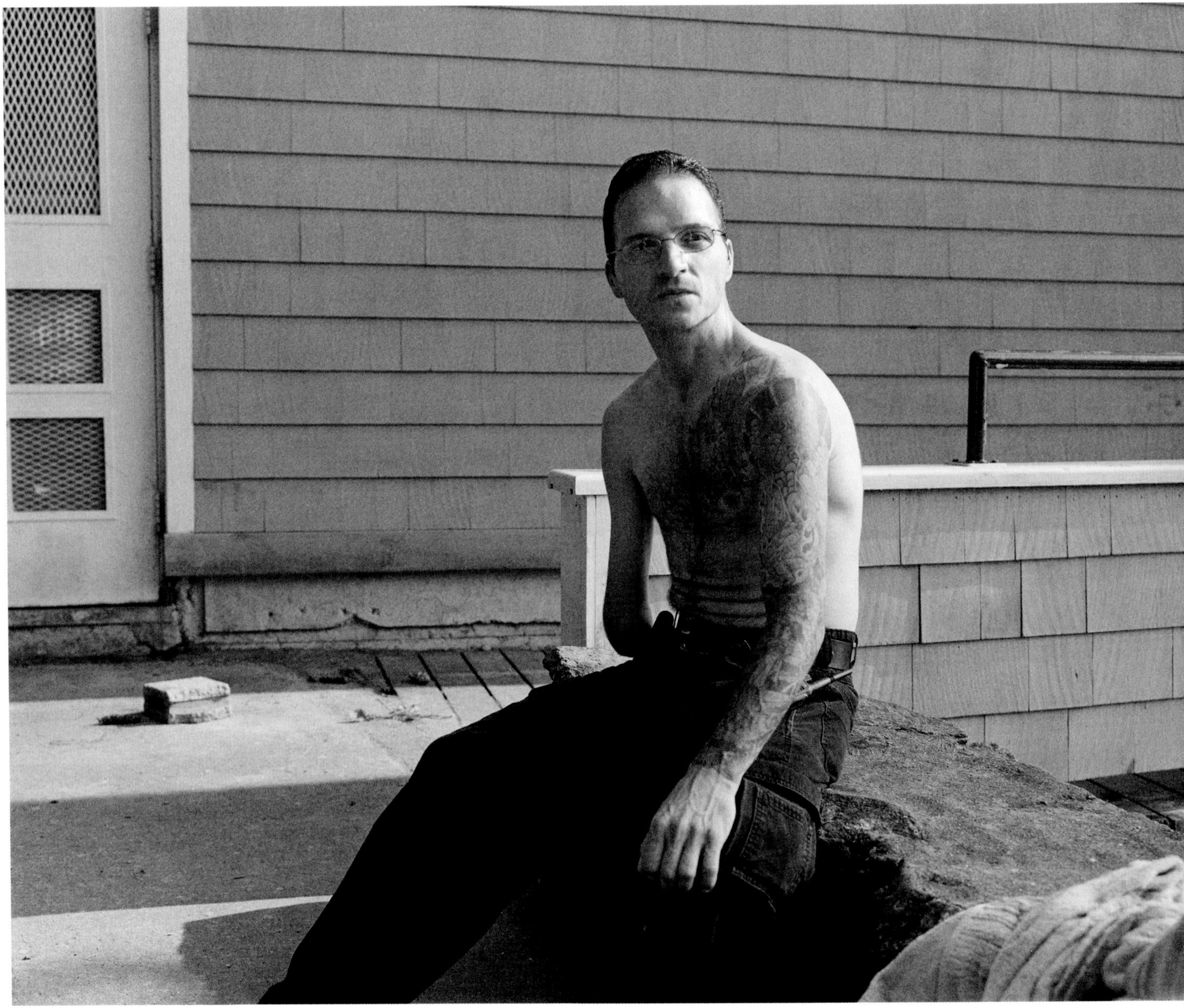

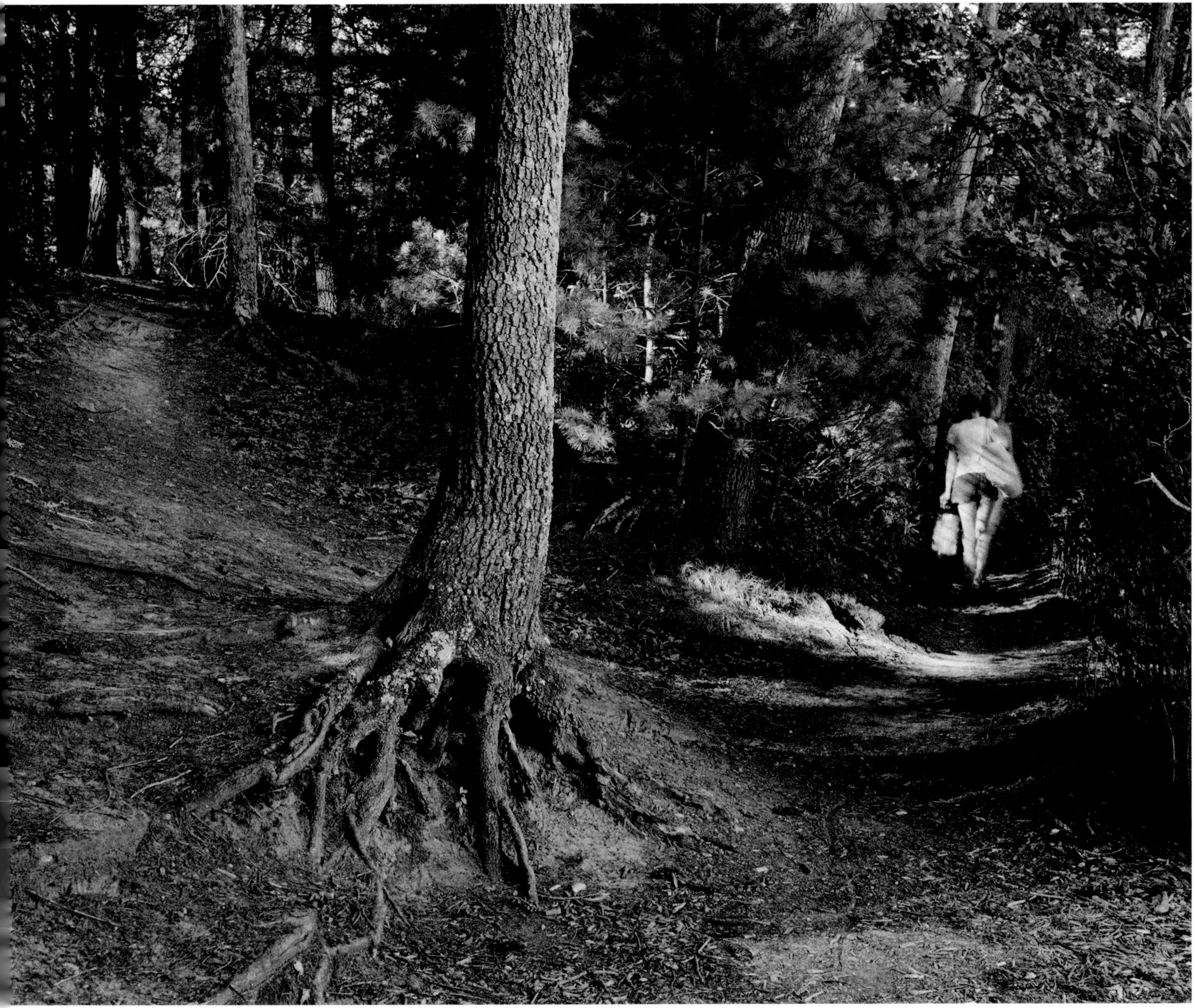

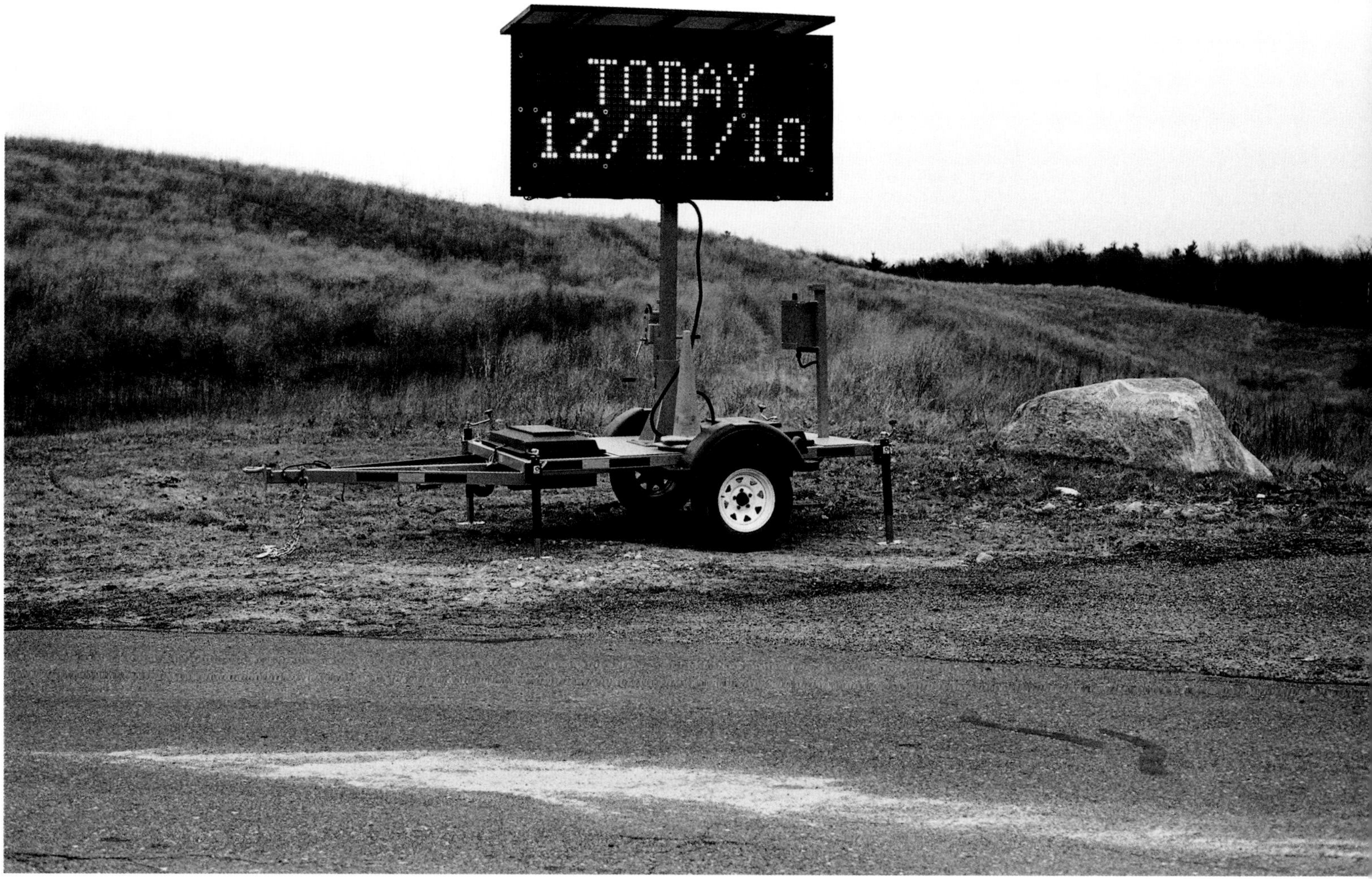
TODAY
12/11/10

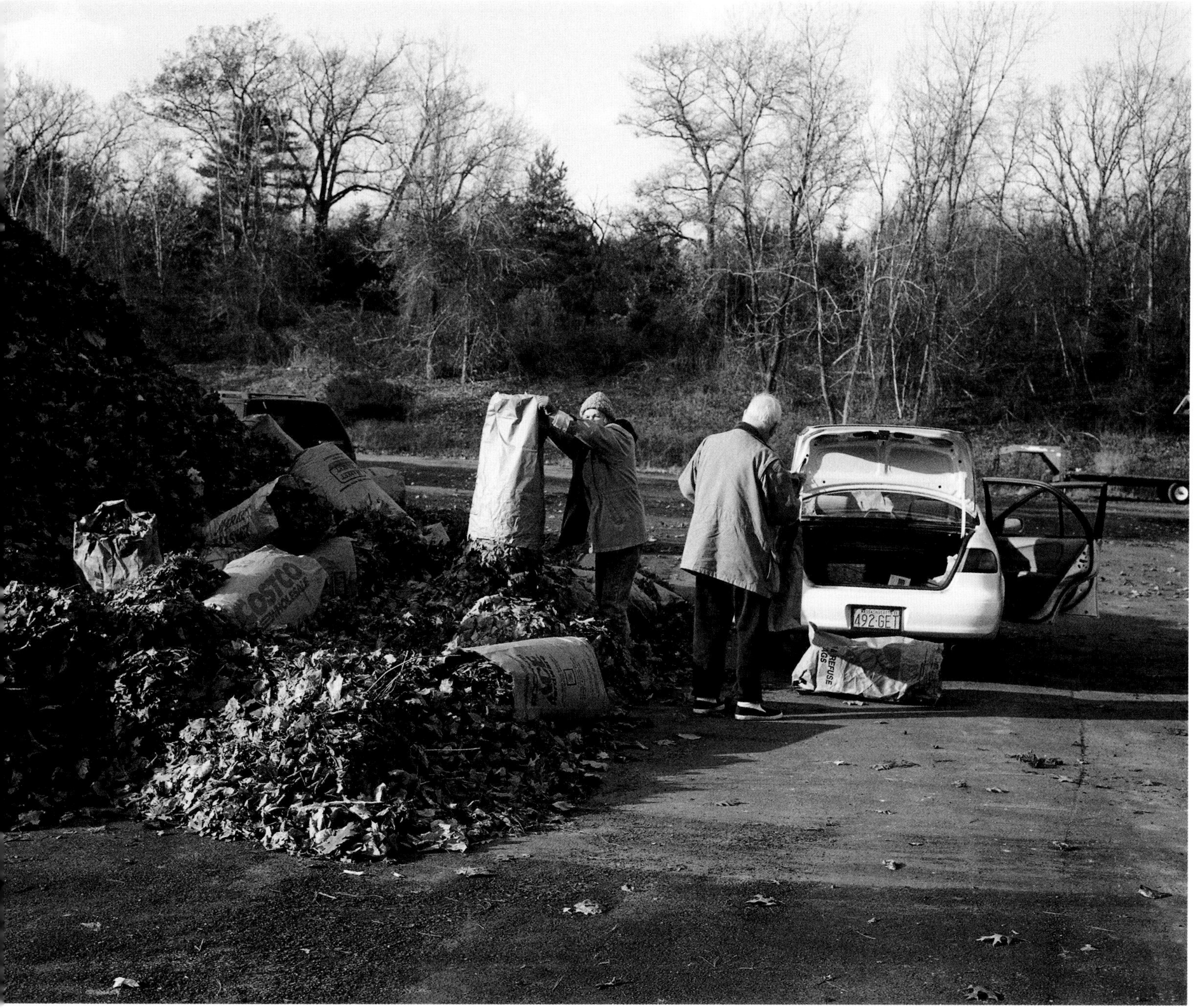
492·GET
REFUSE

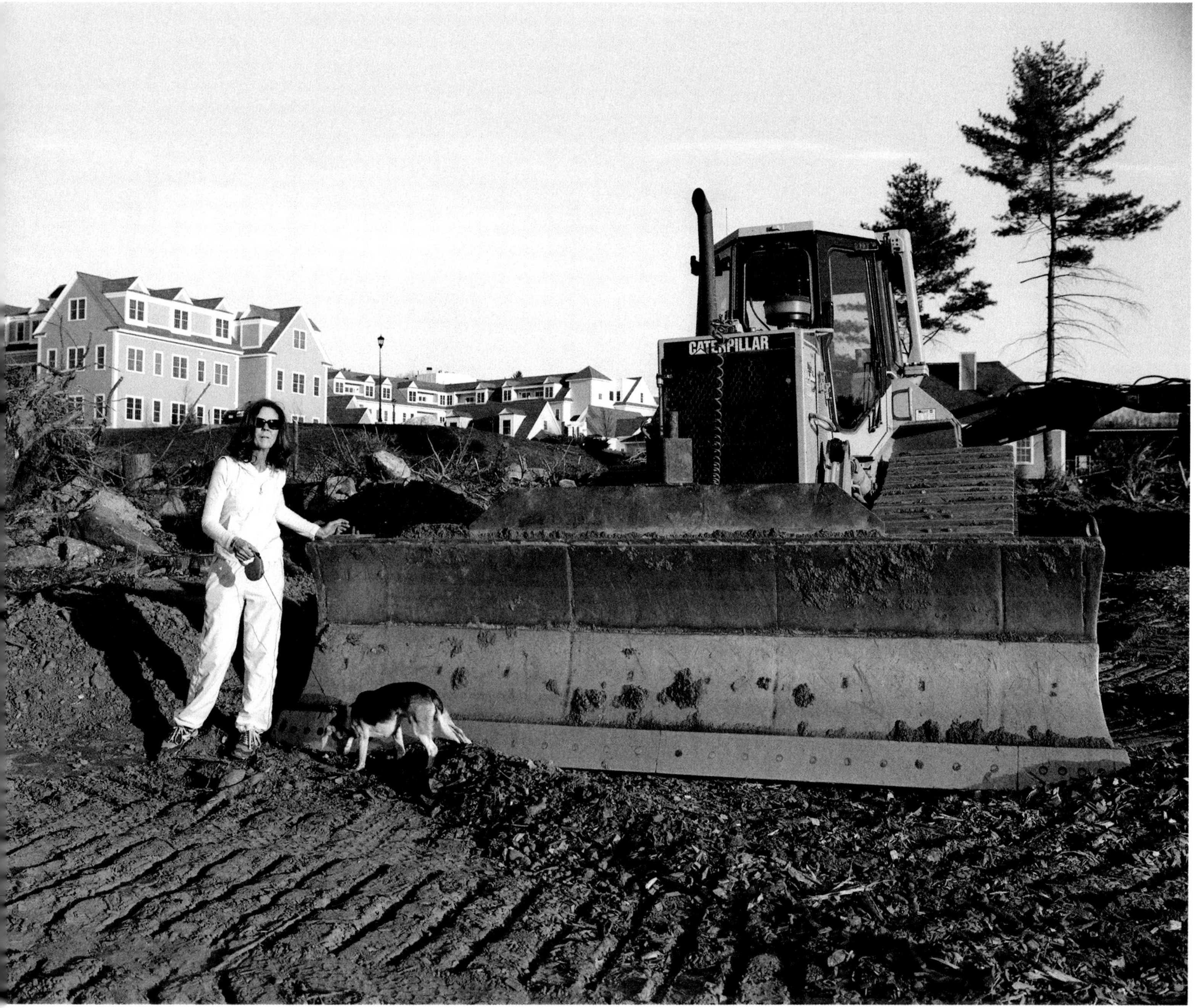
CATERPILLAR

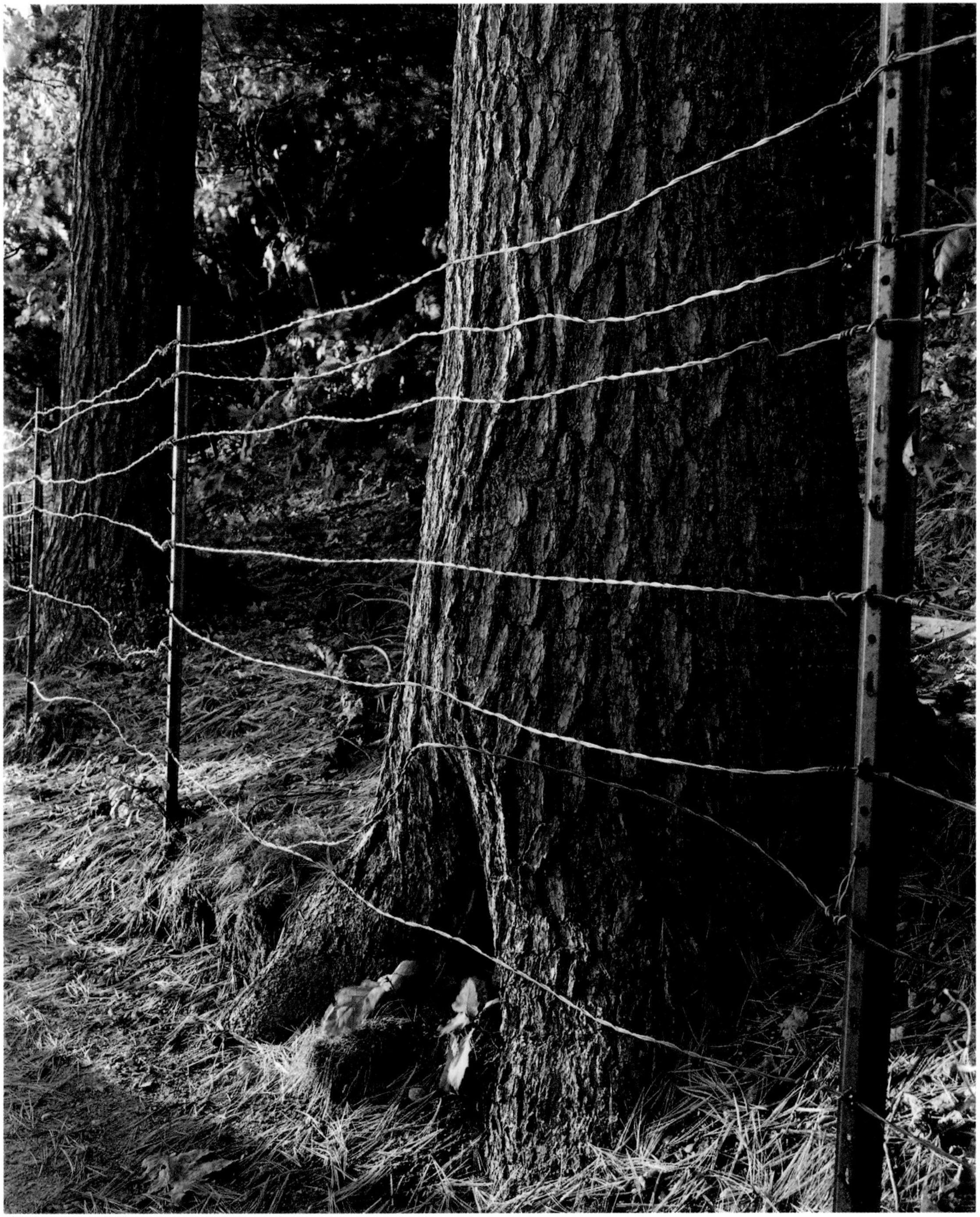

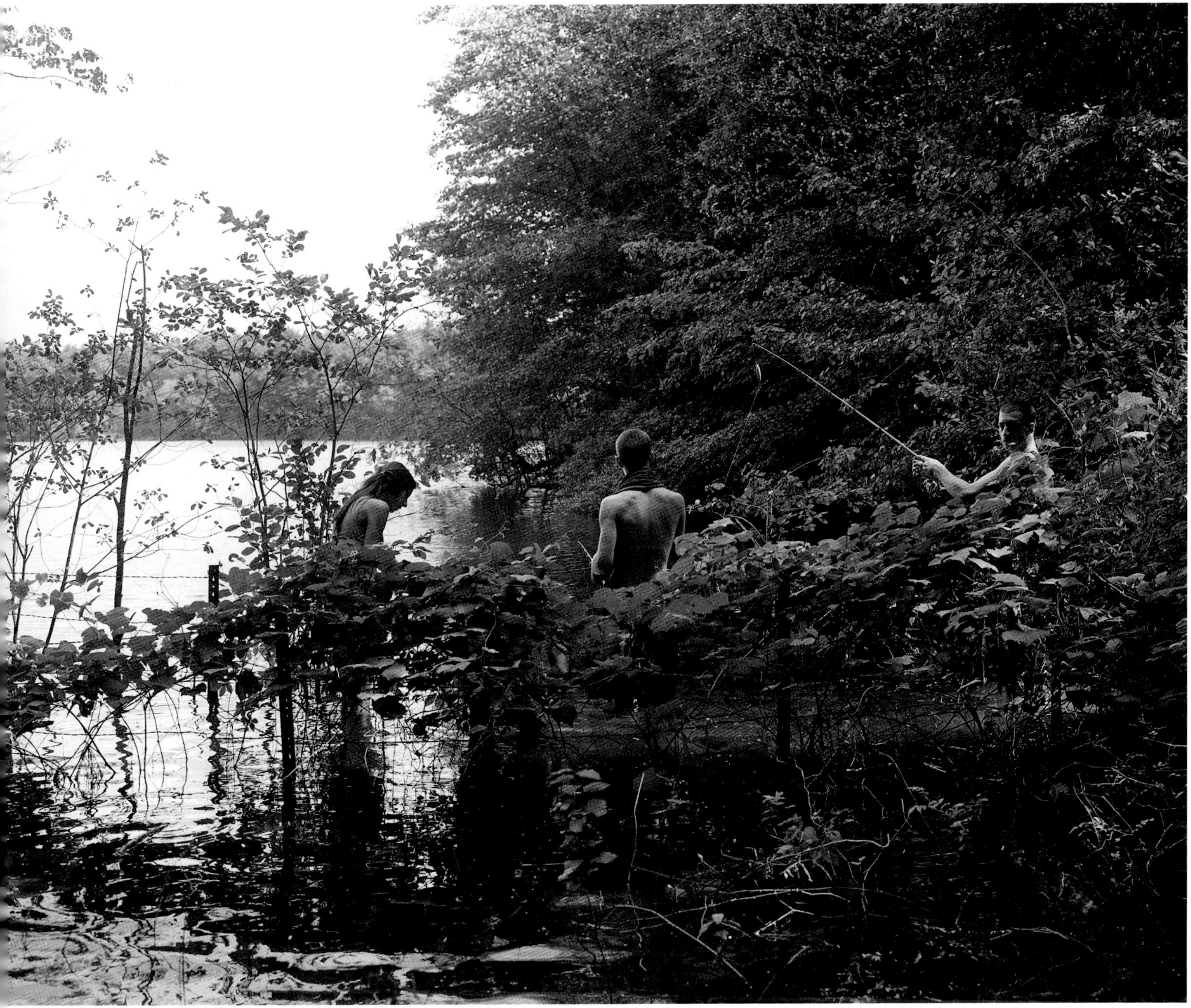

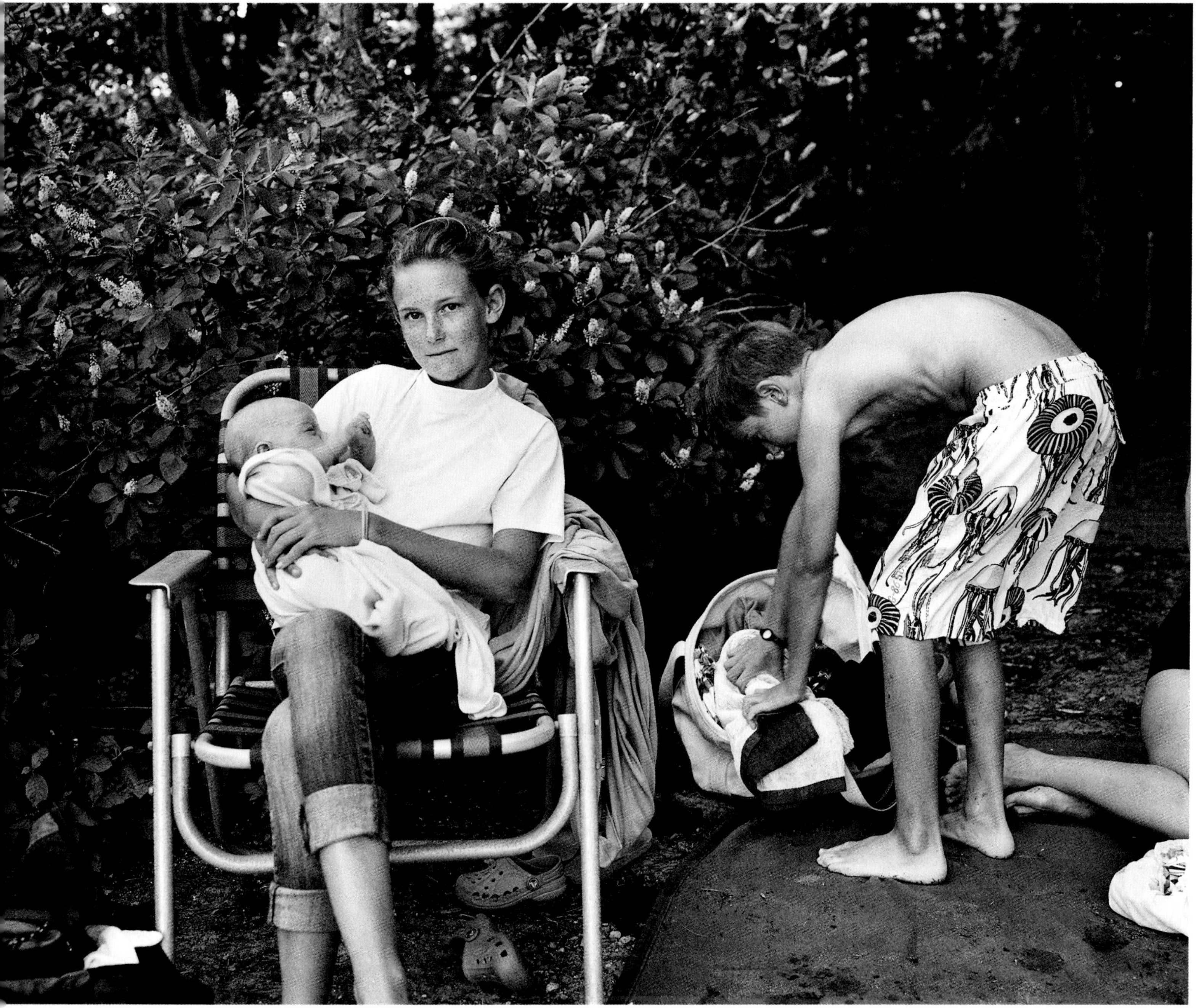

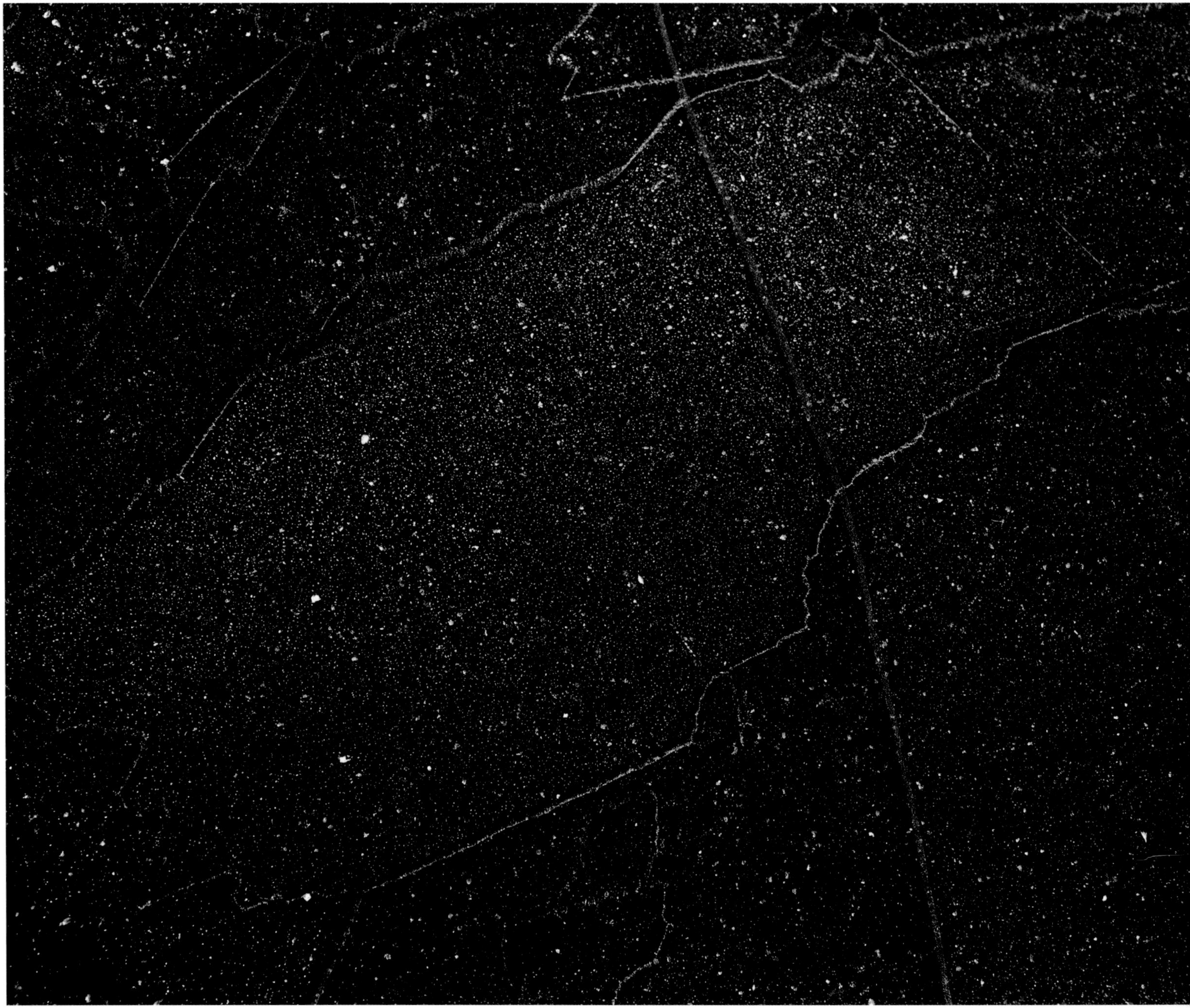

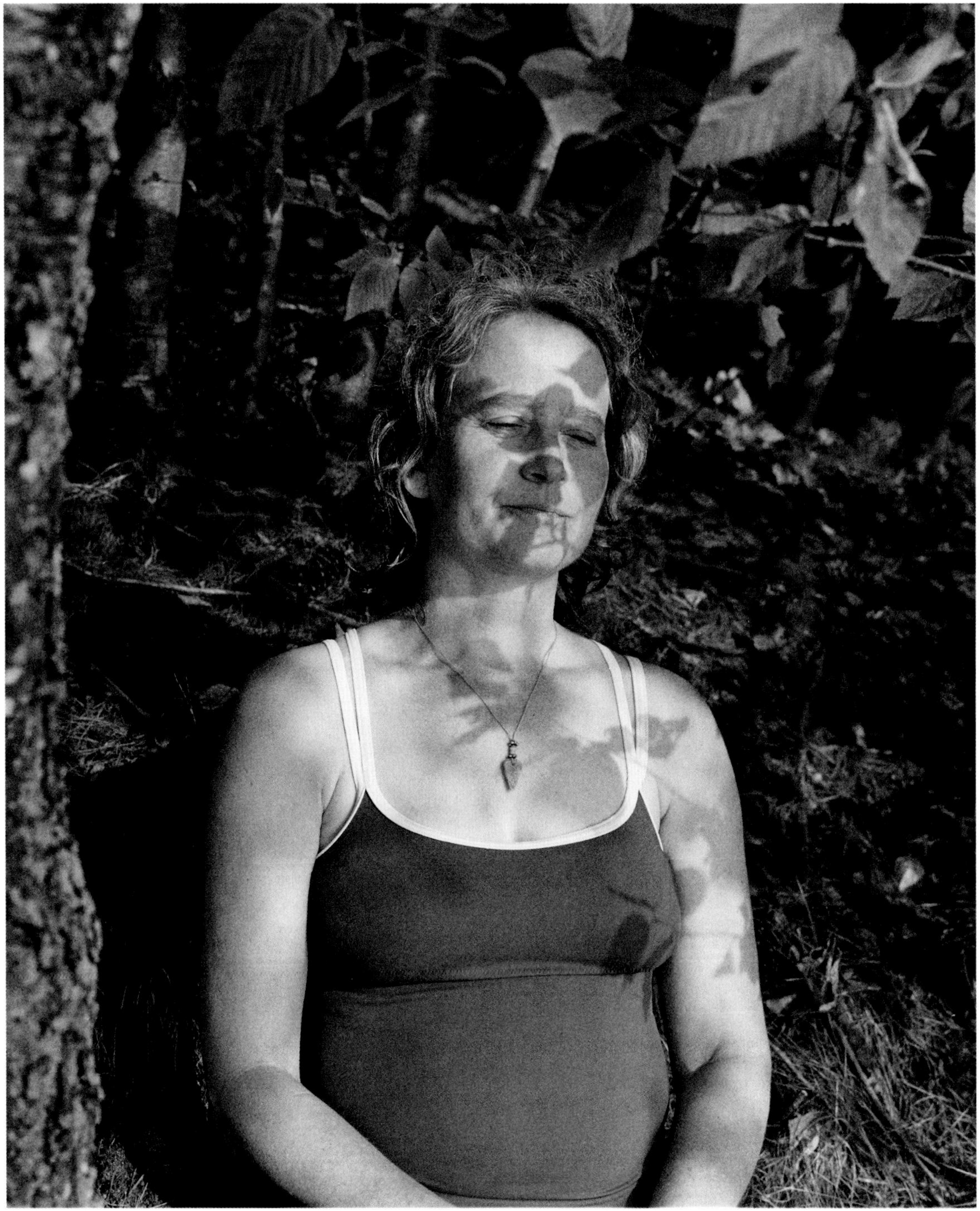

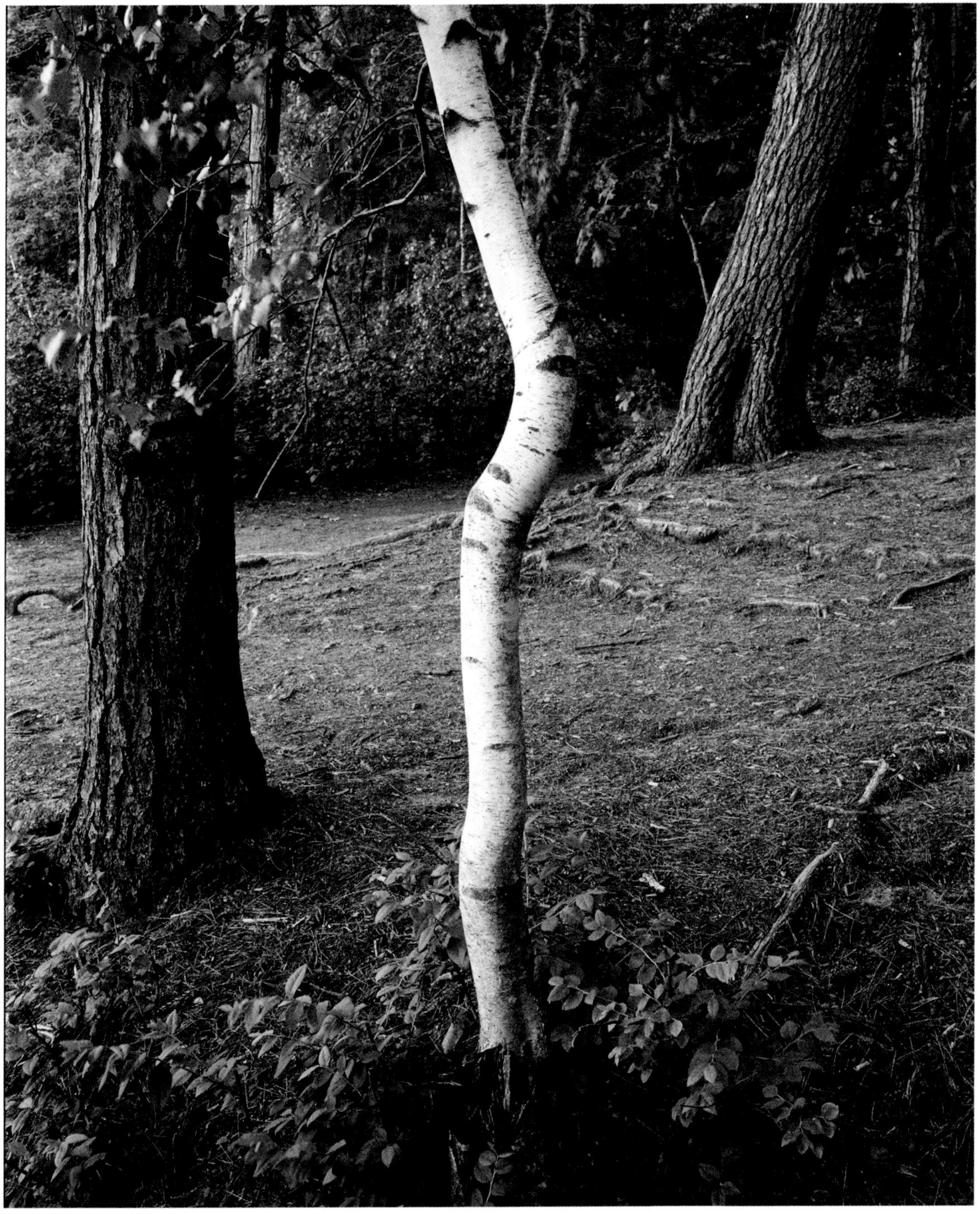

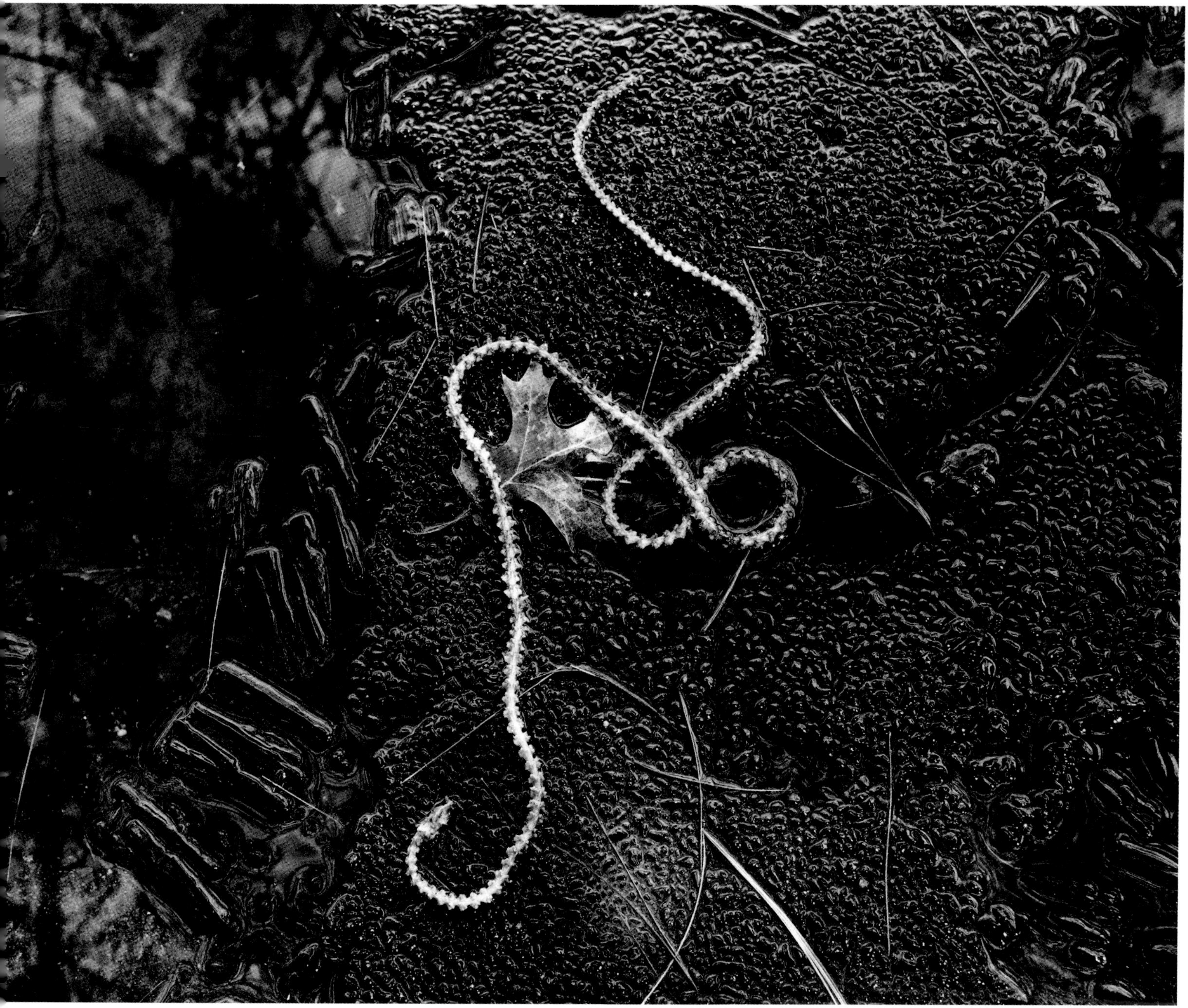

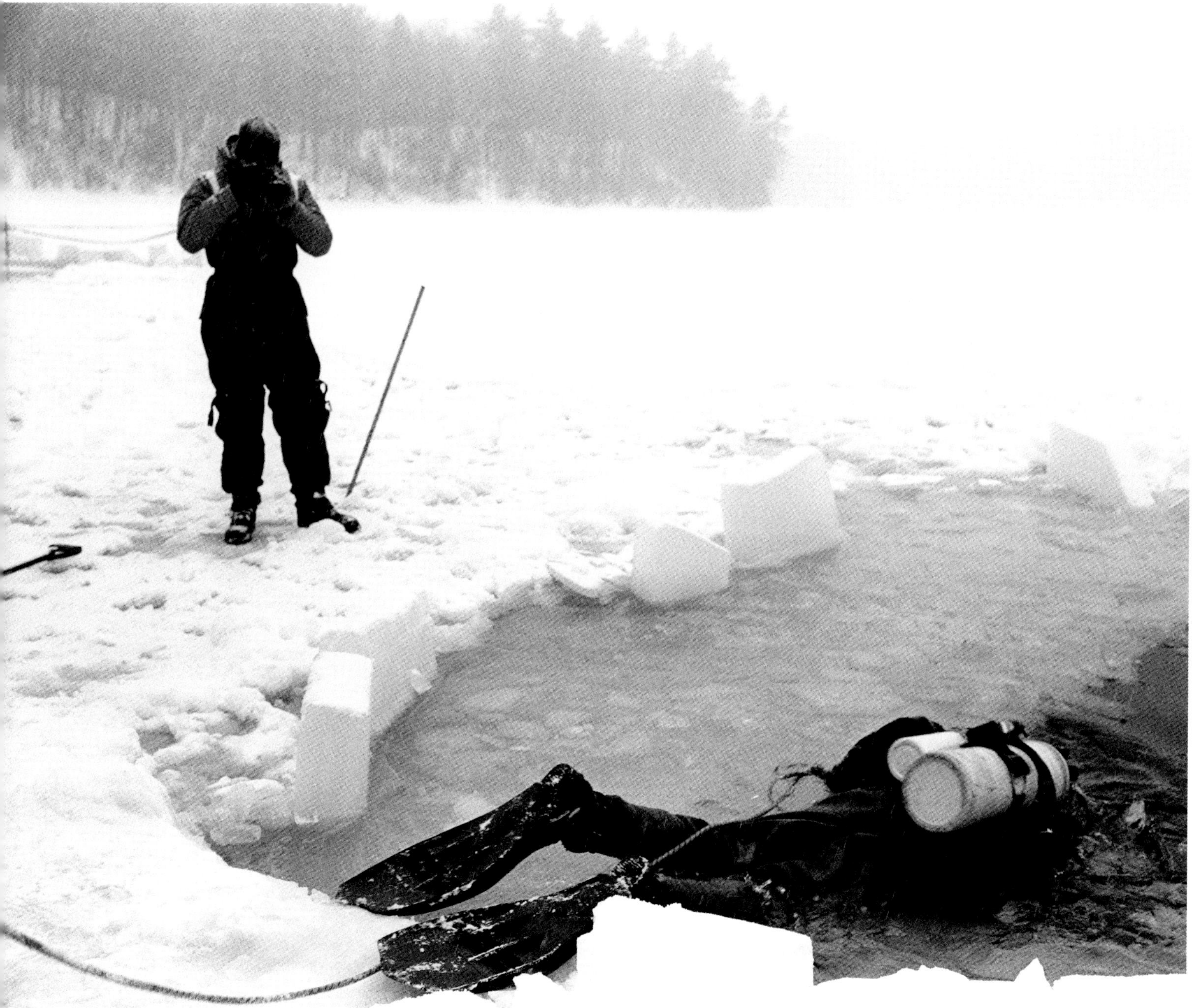

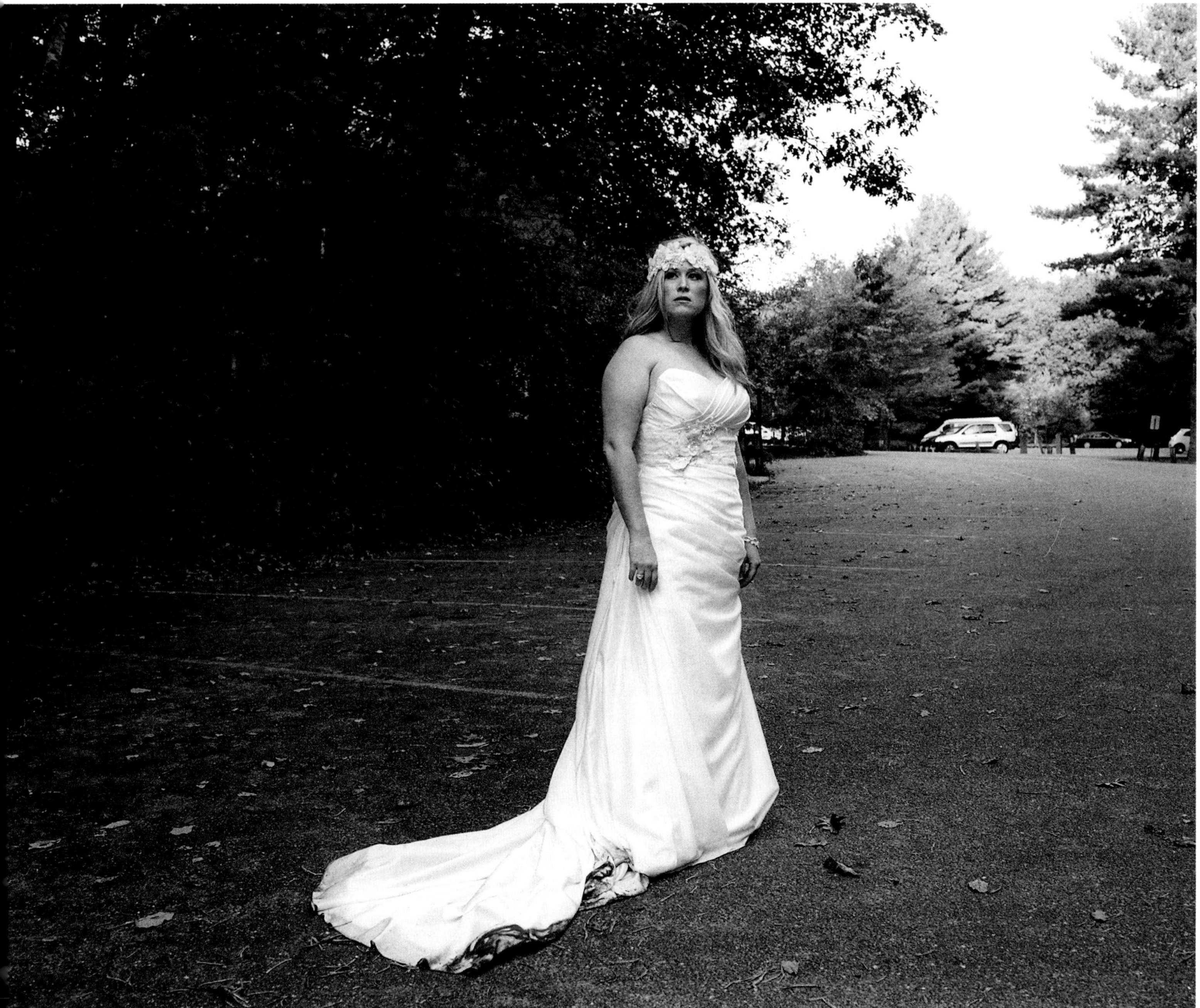

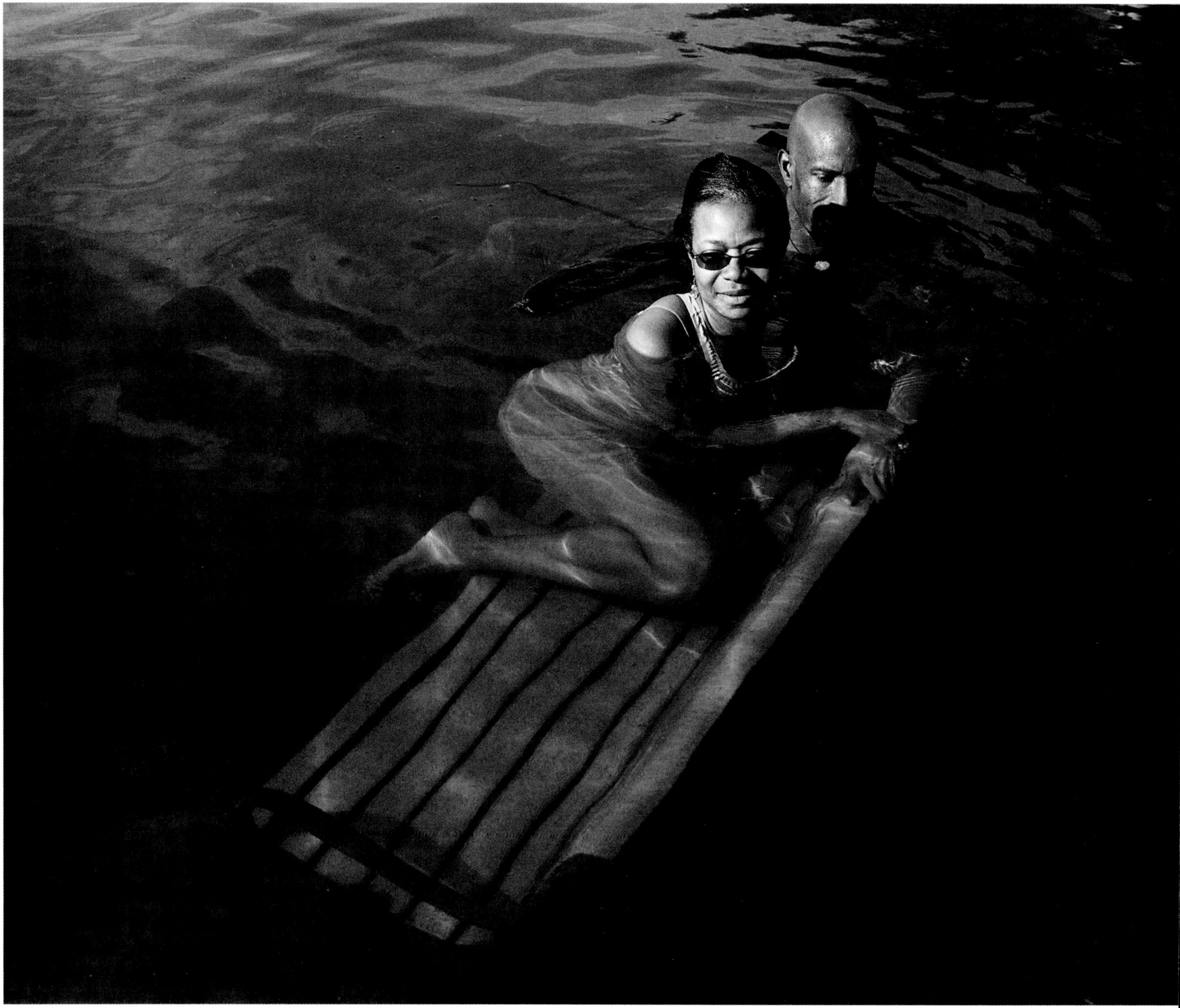

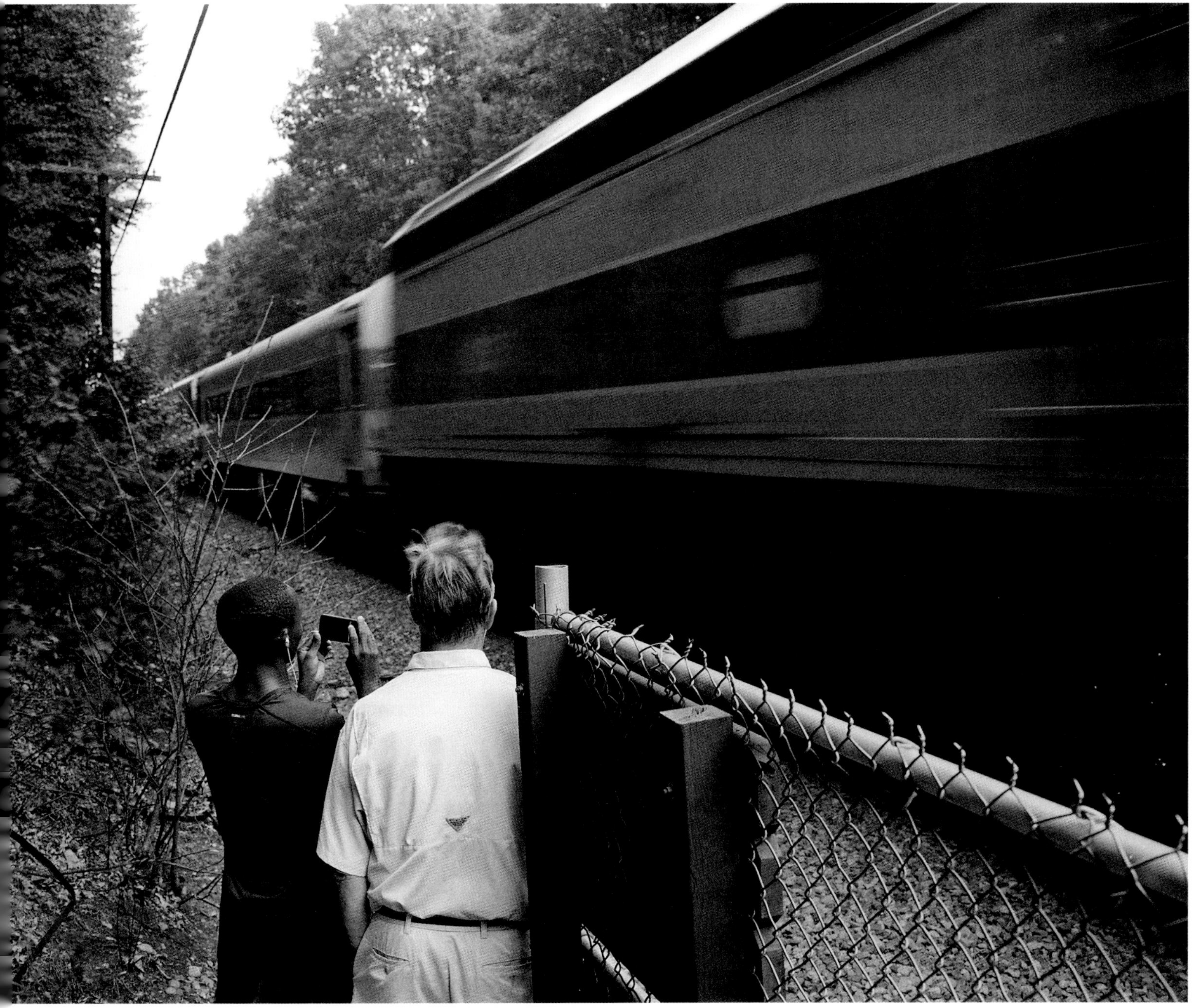

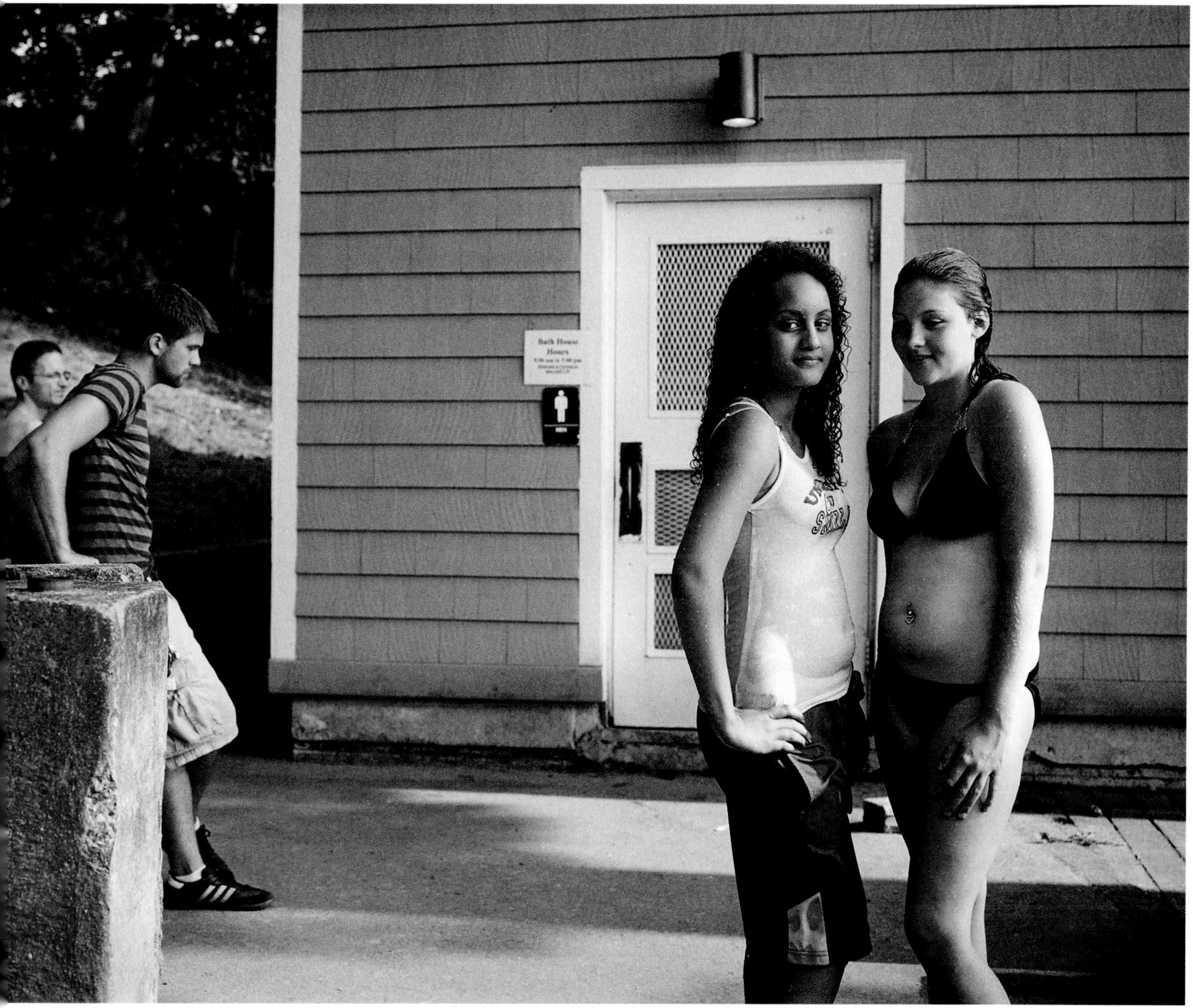
Bath House
Hours
MEN

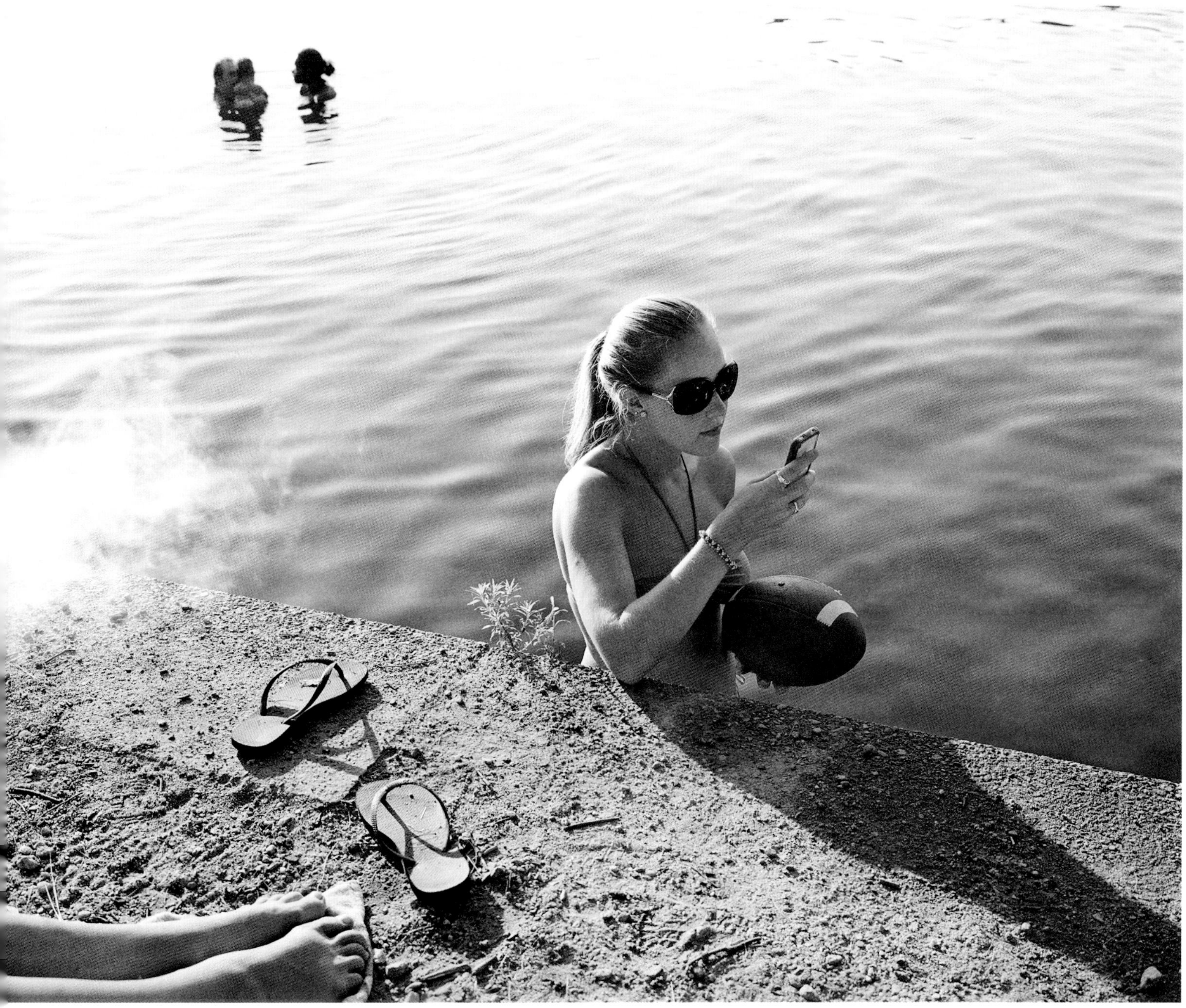

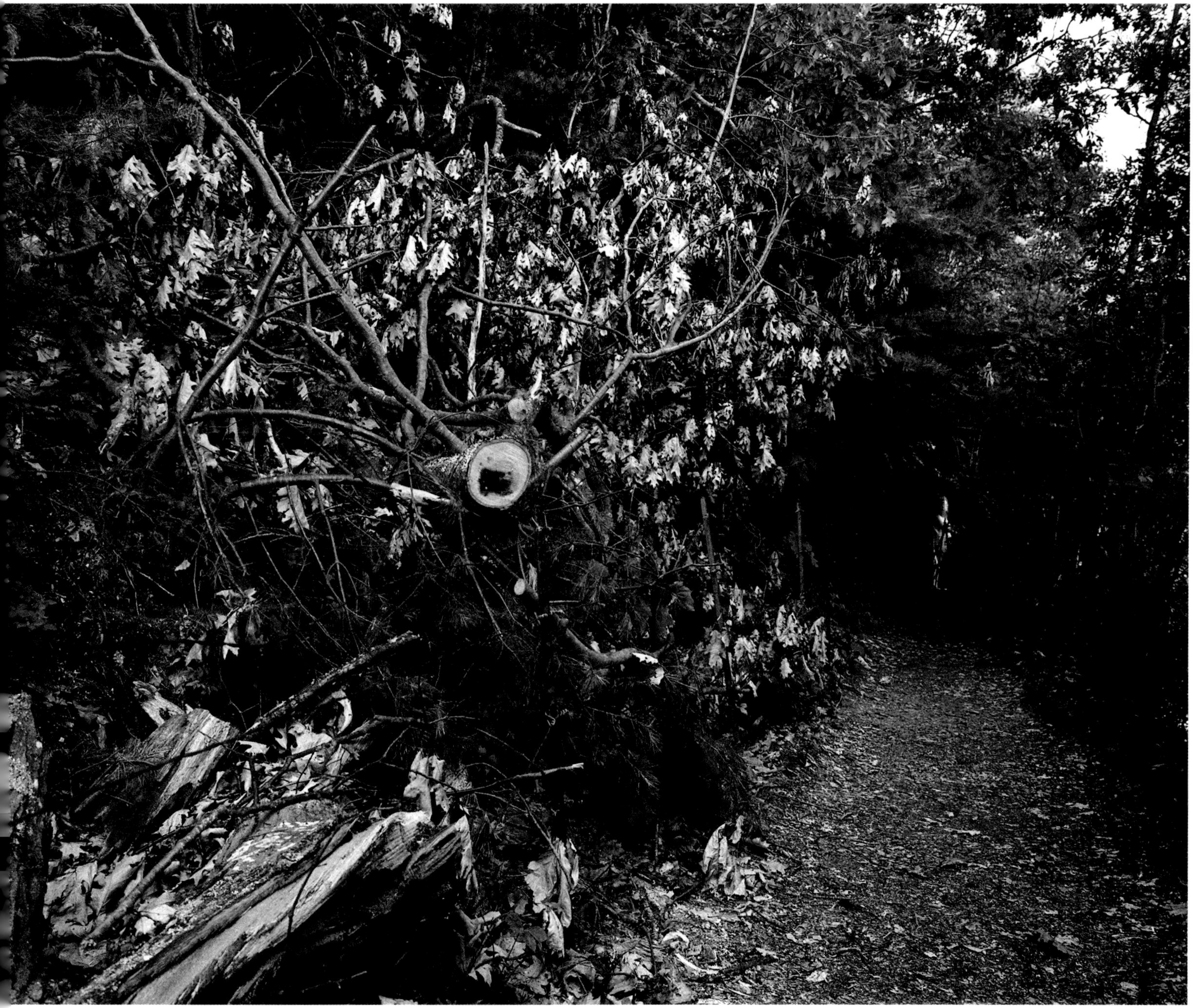

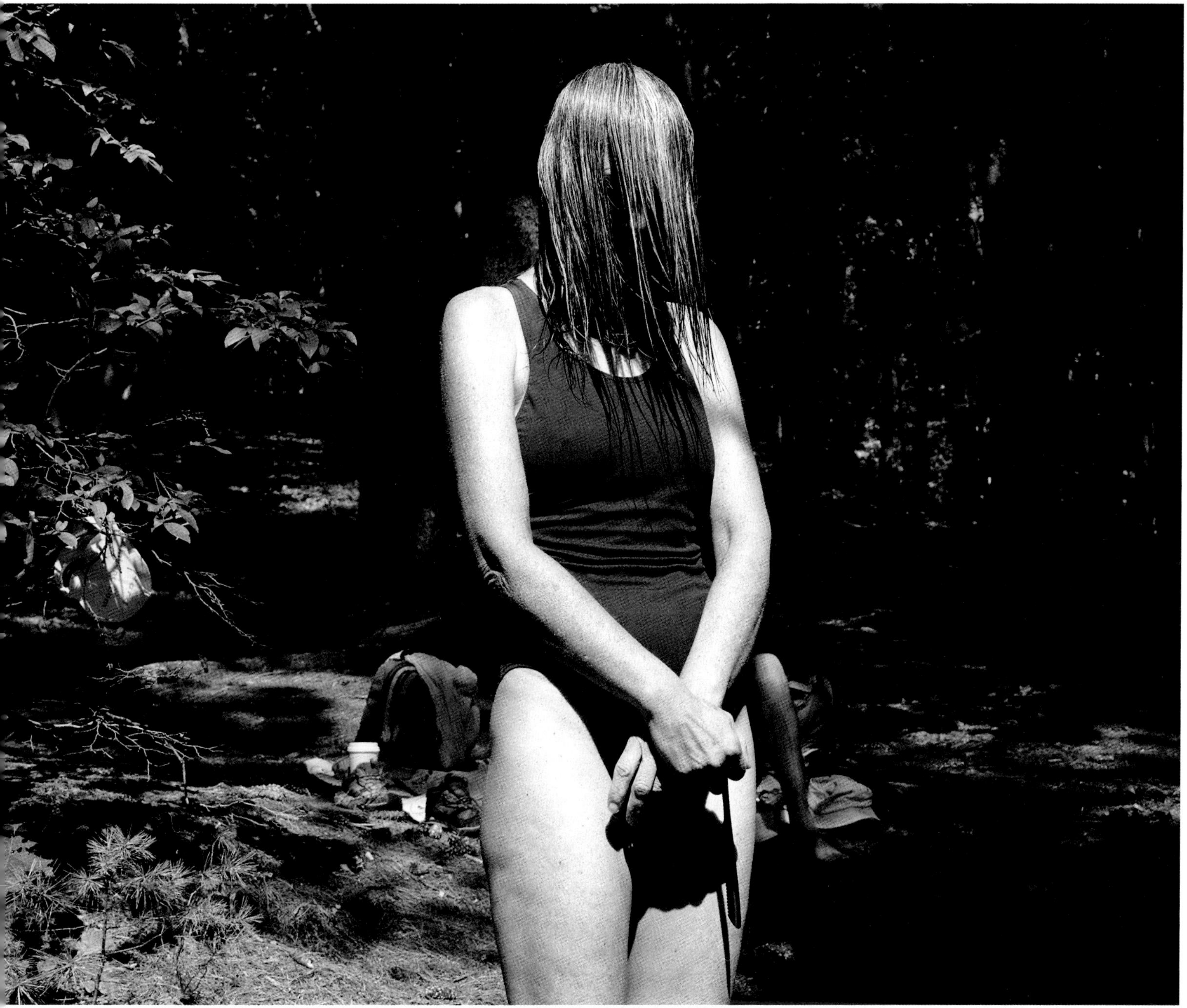

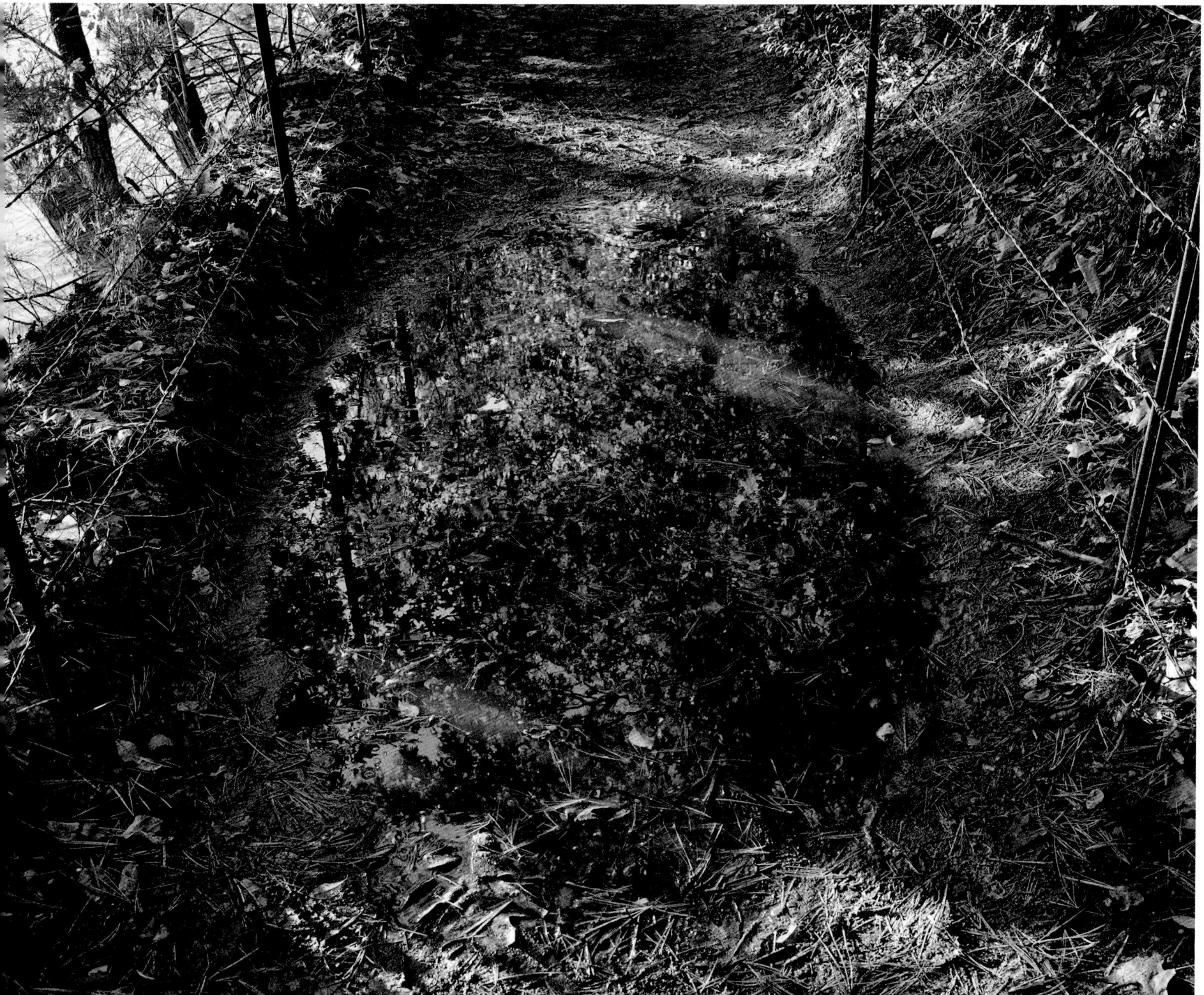

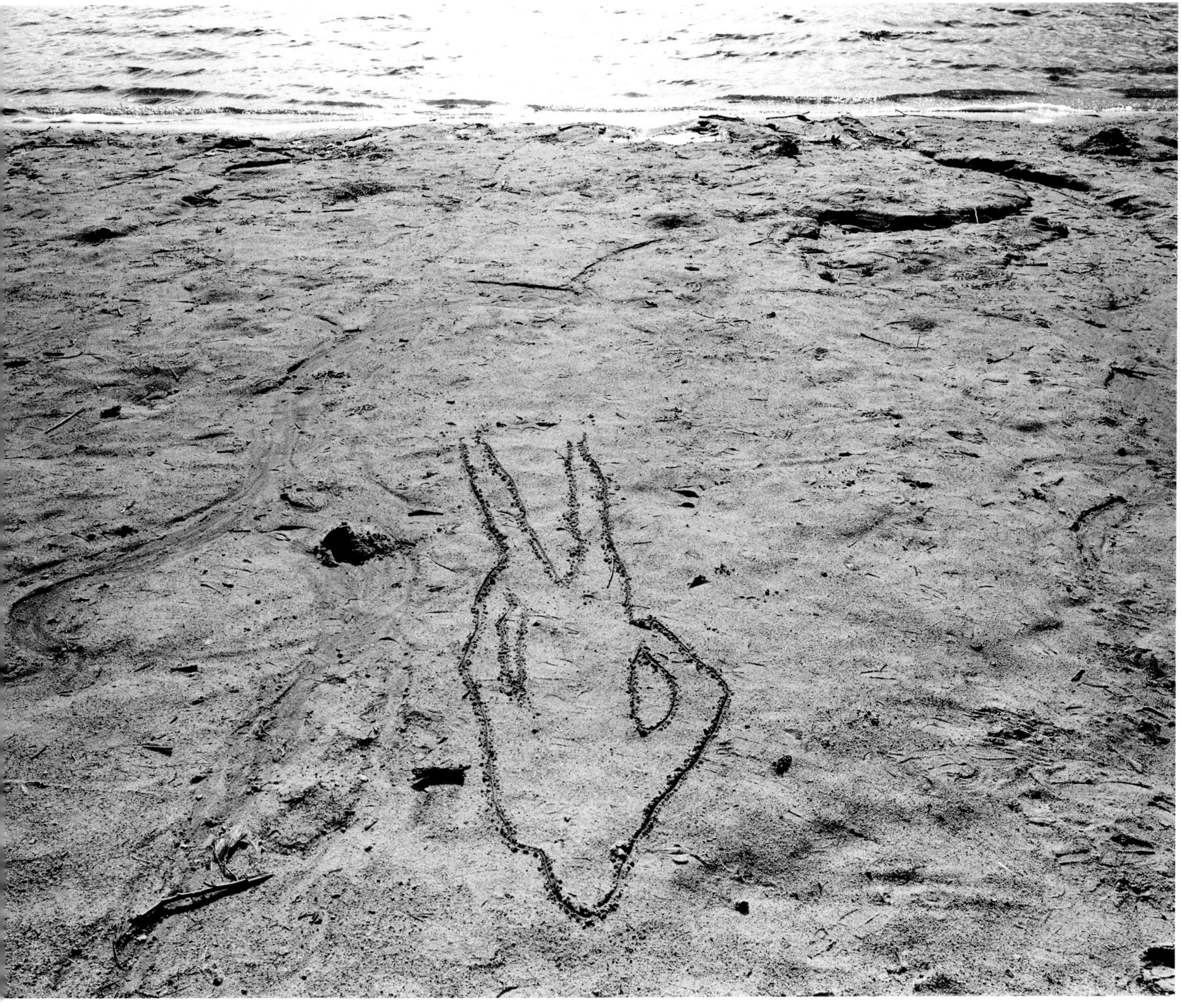

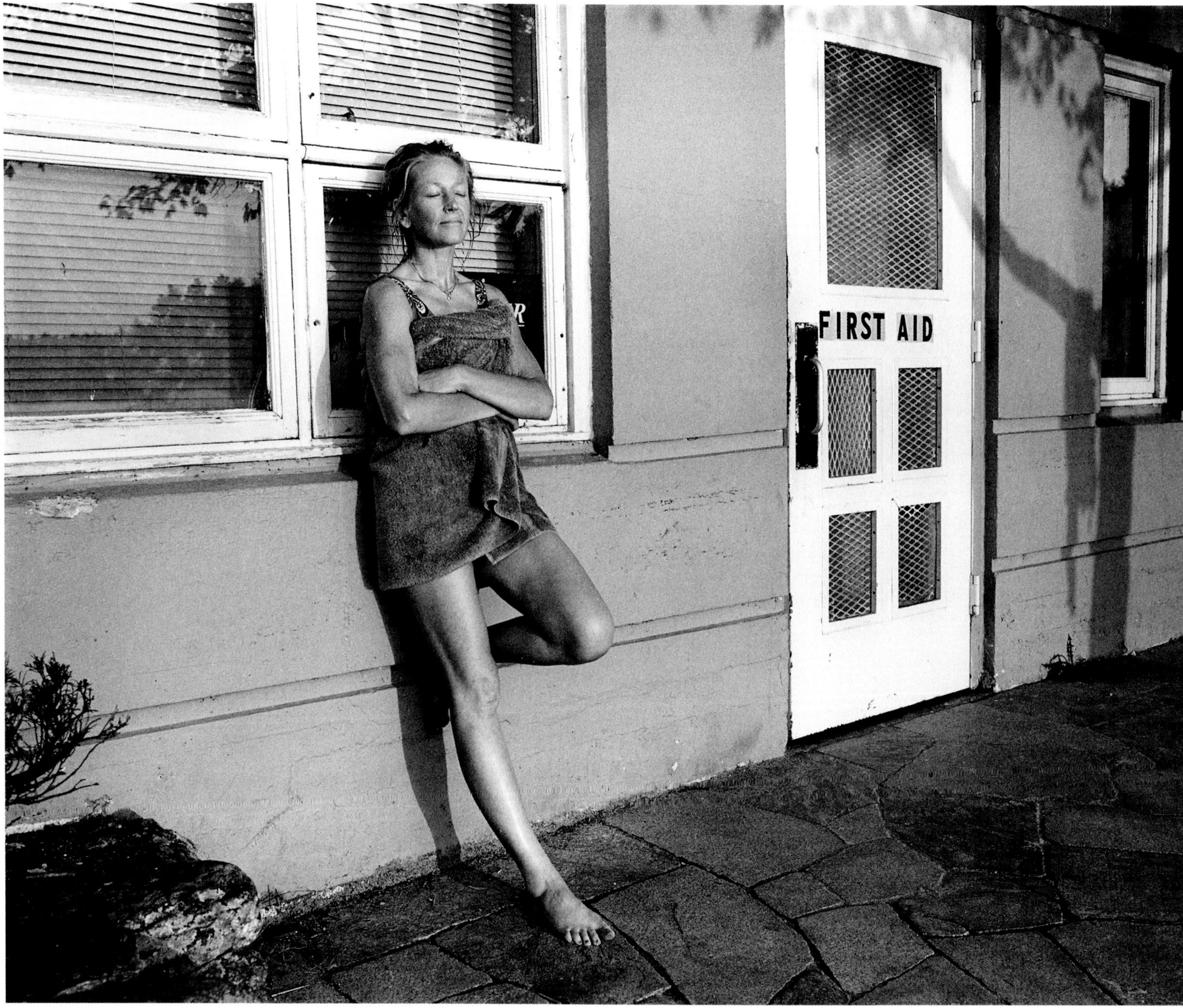
FIRST AID

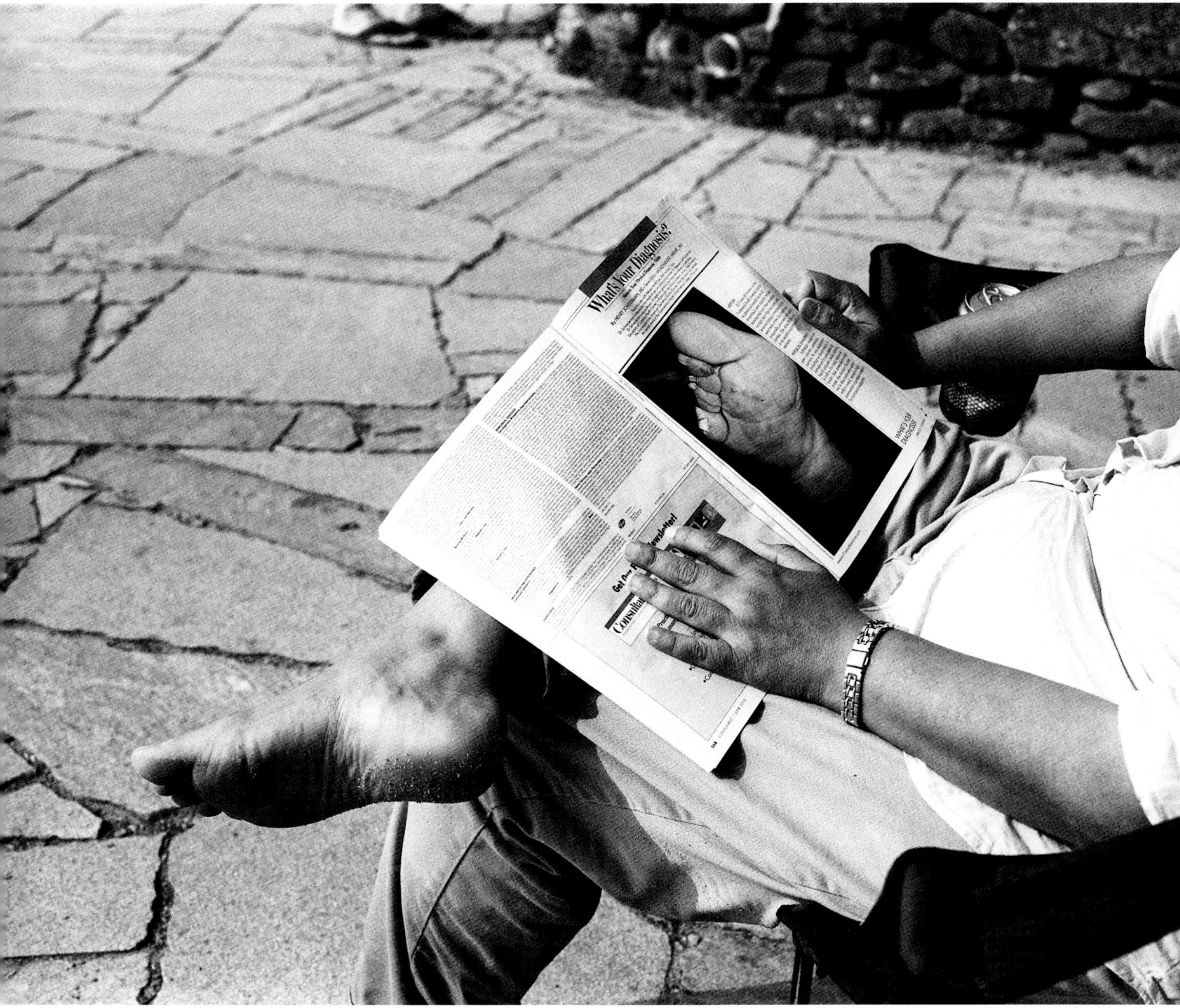
What's Your Diagnosis?

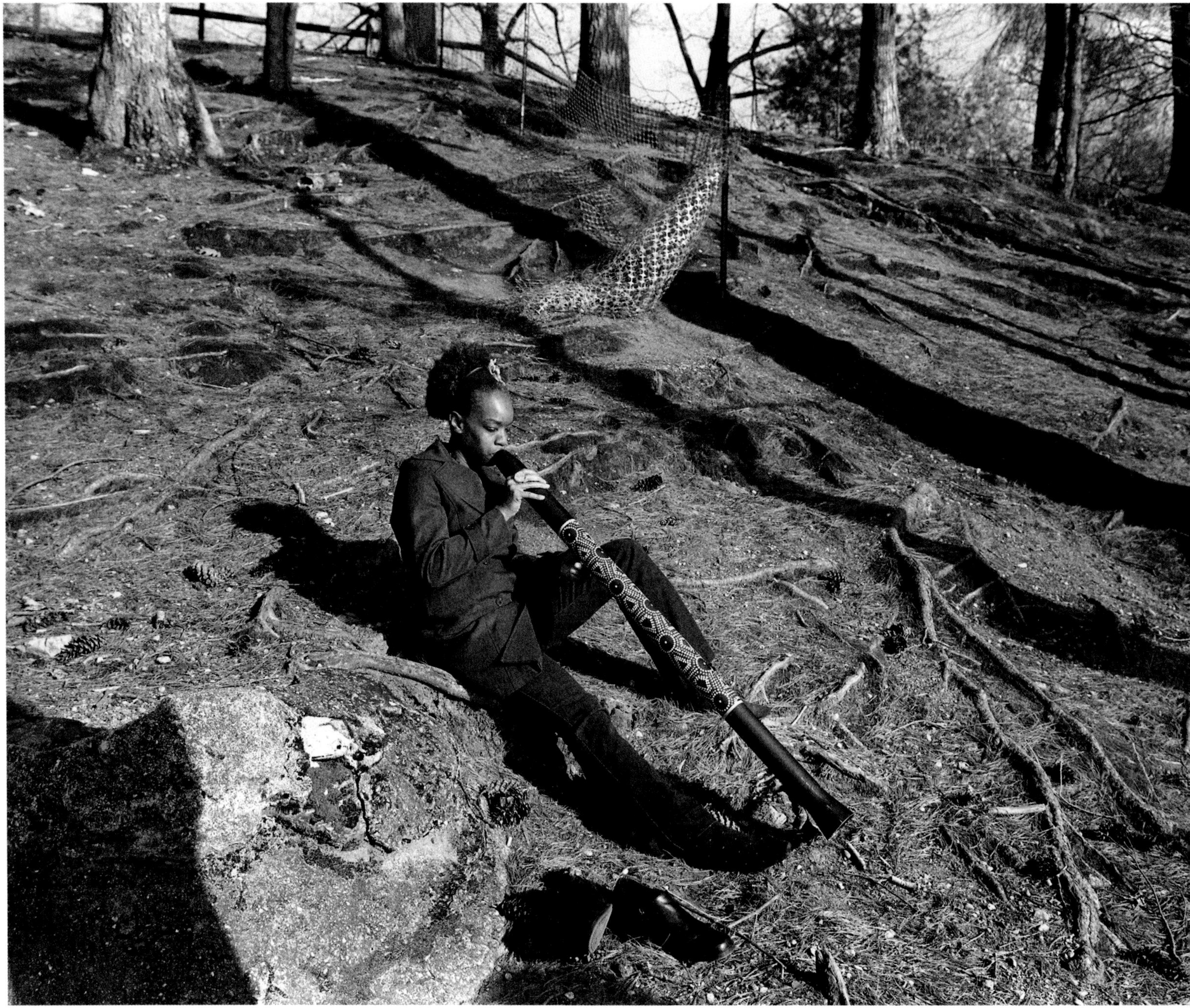

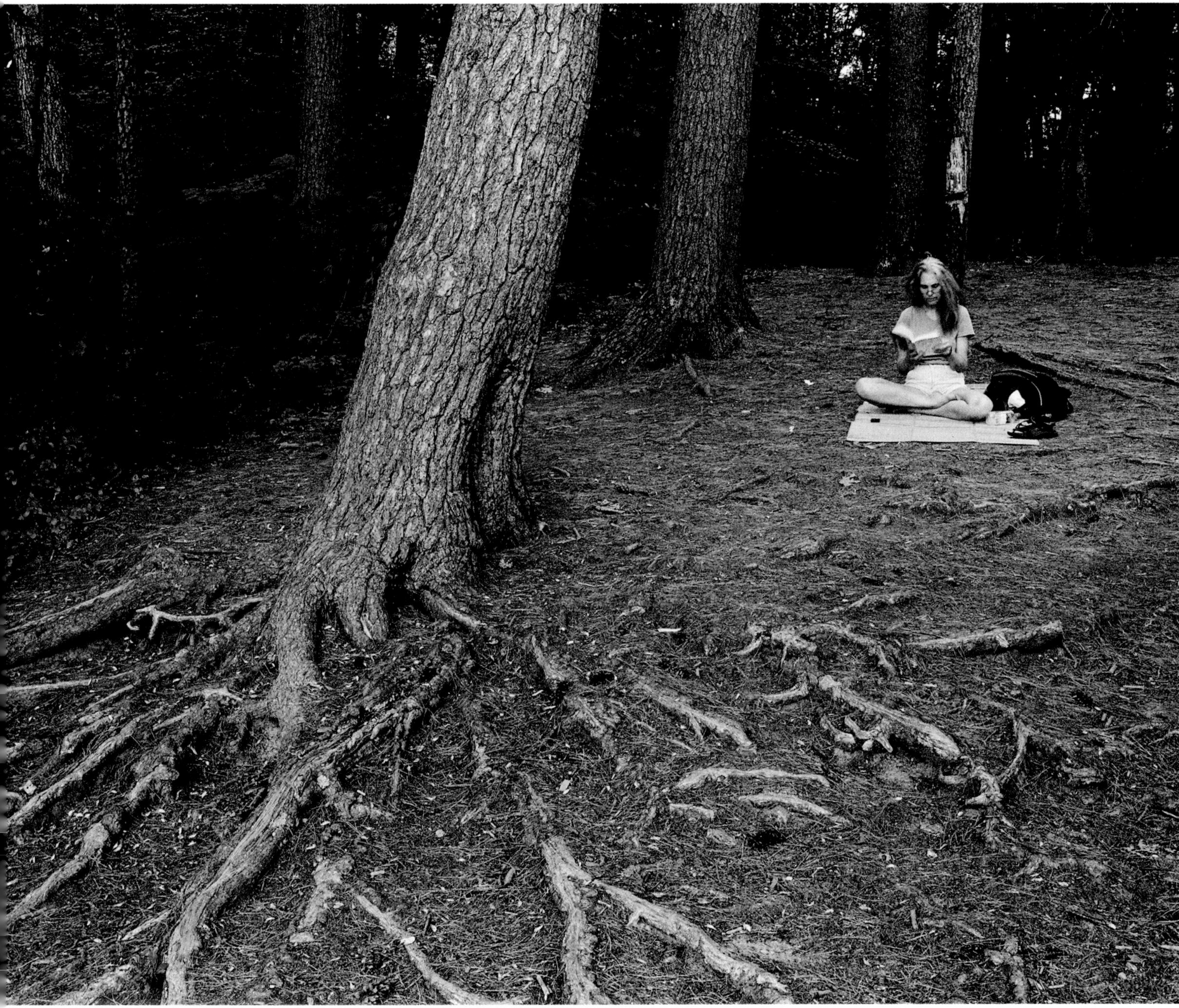

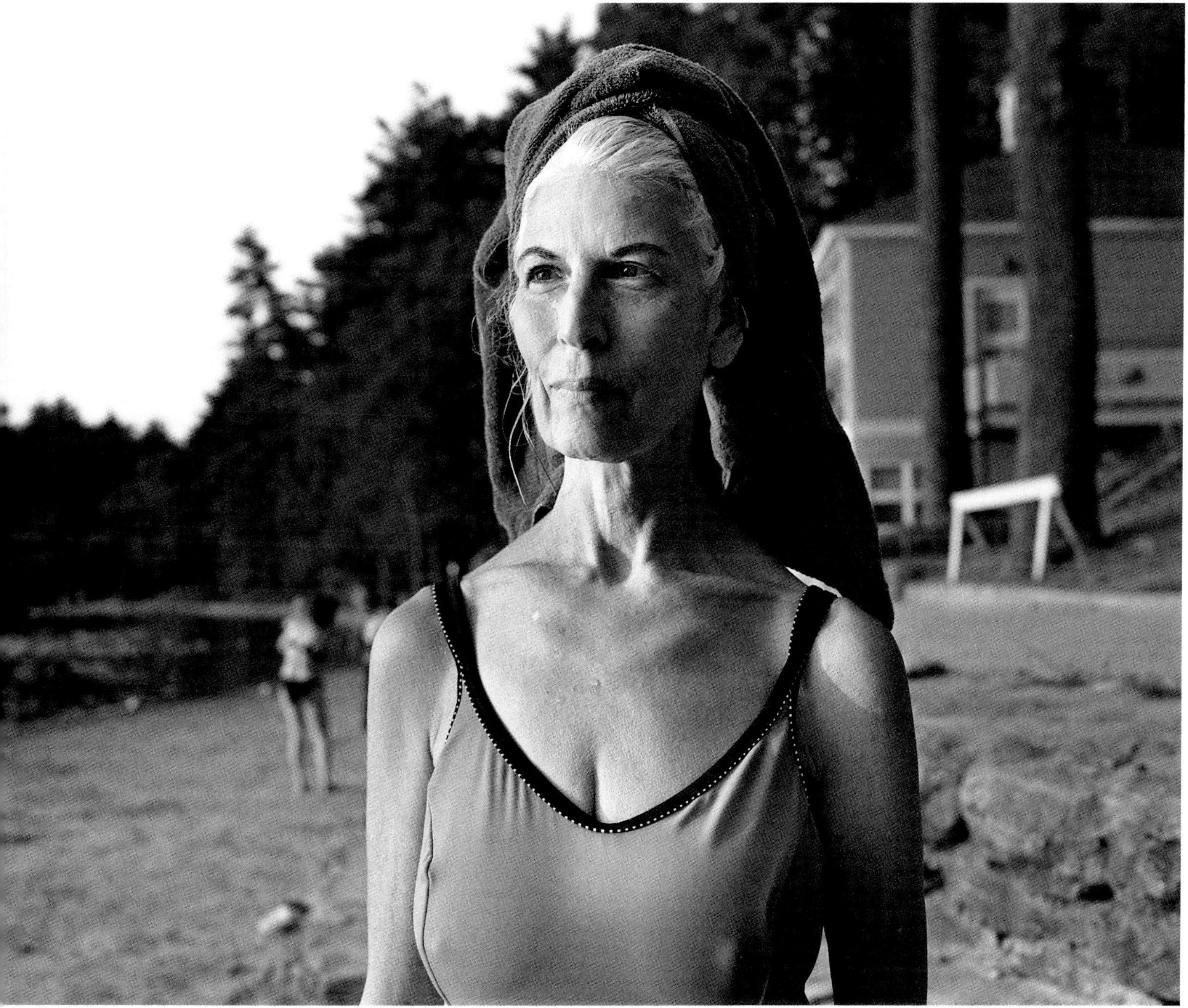

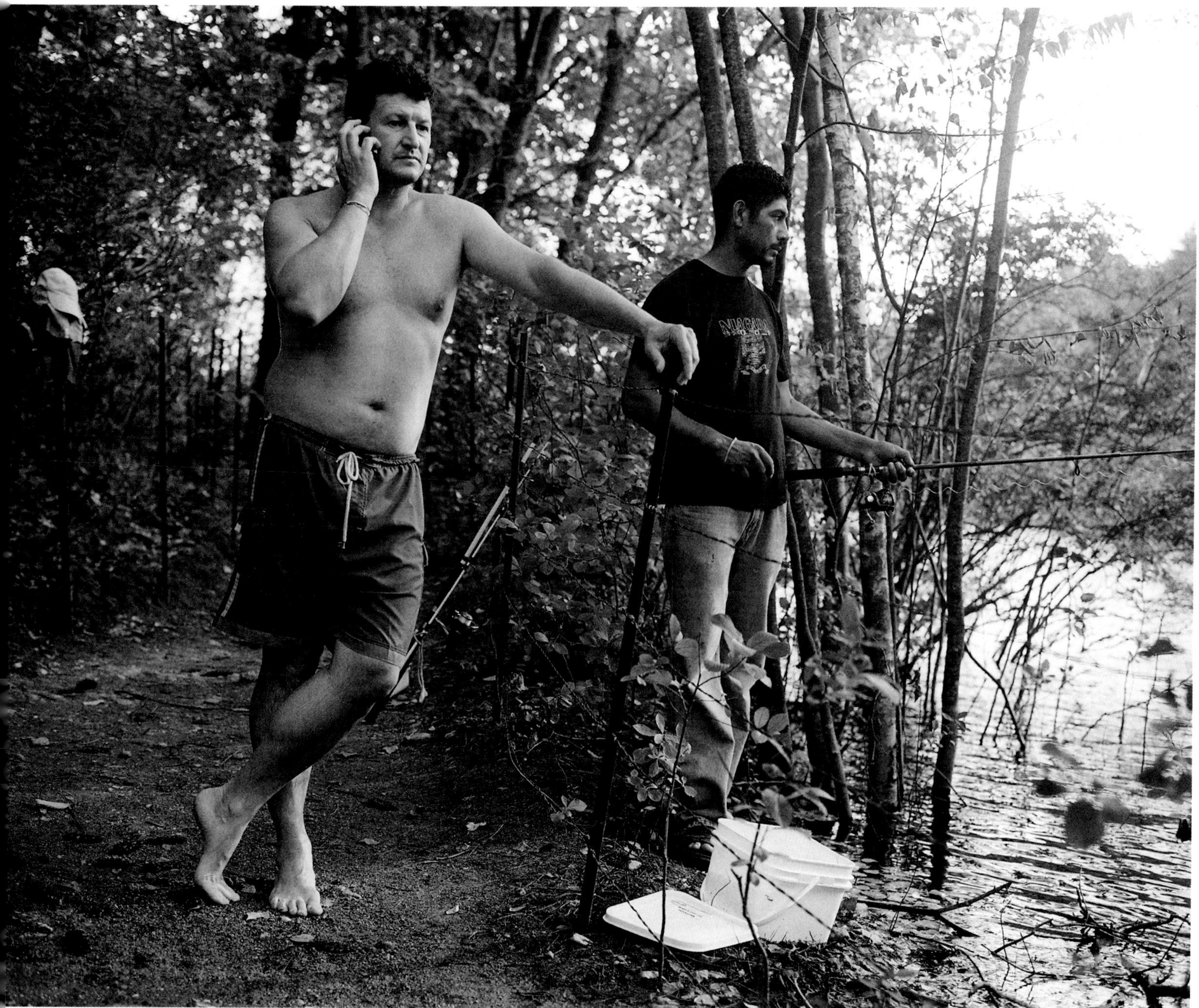

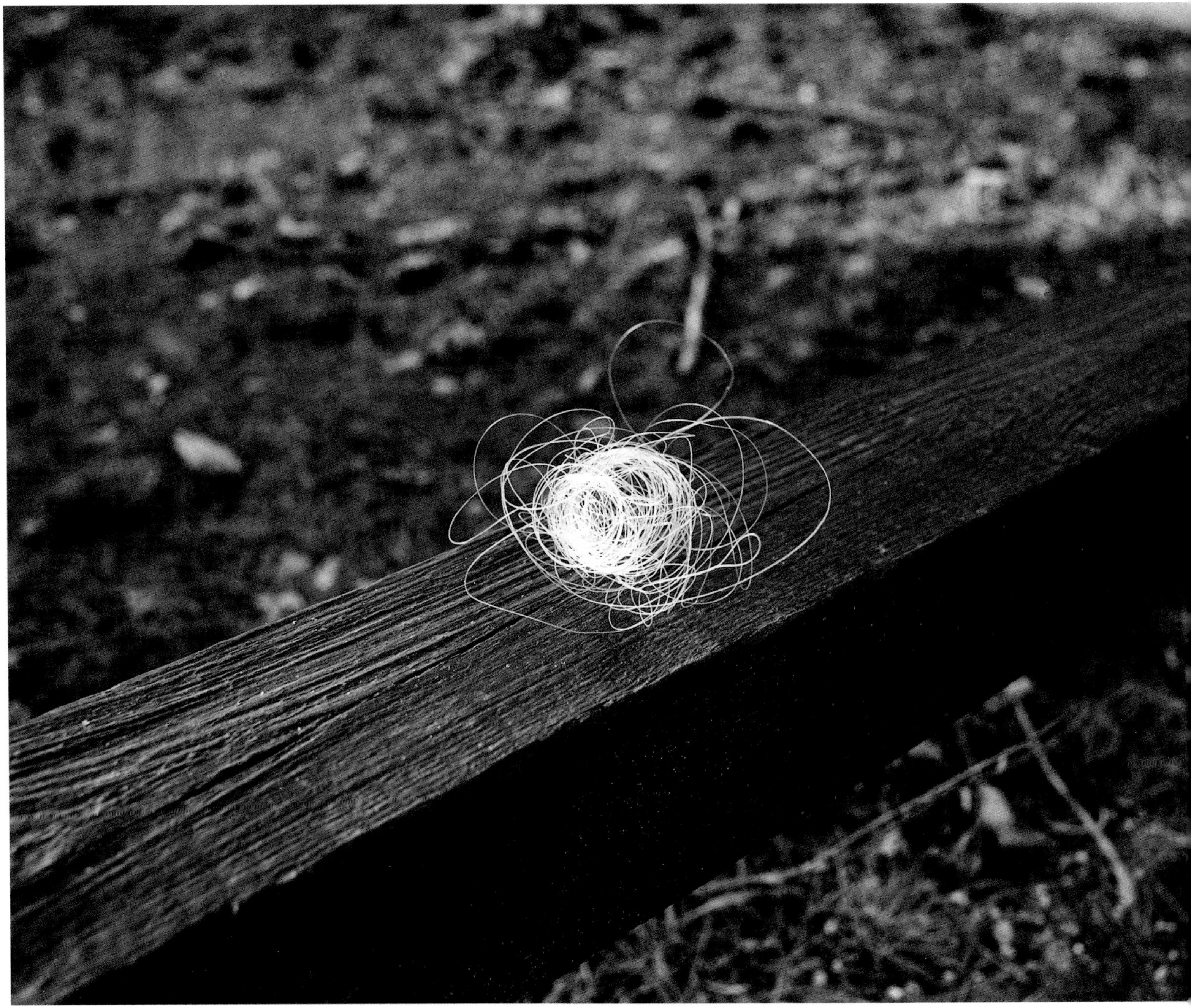

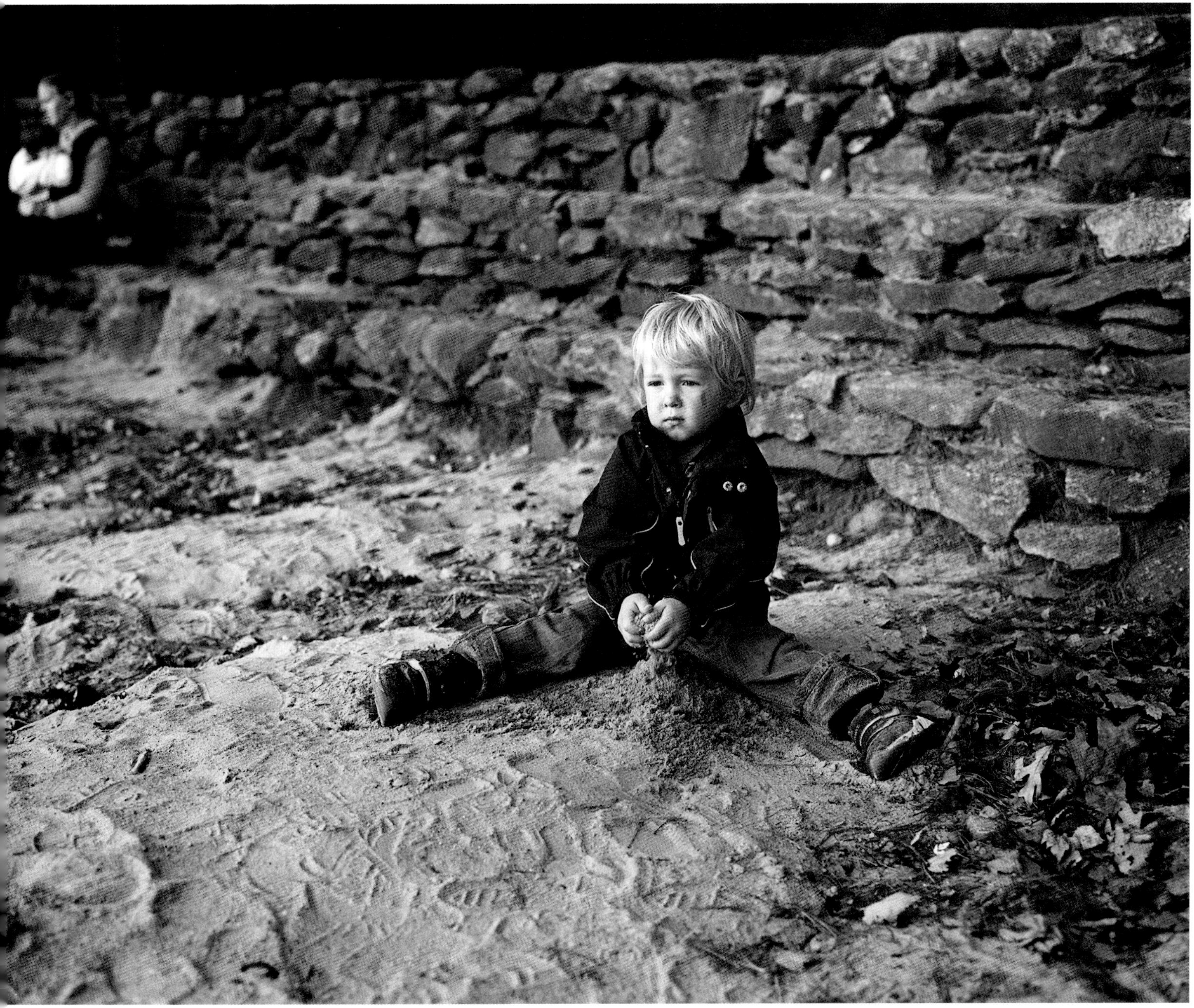

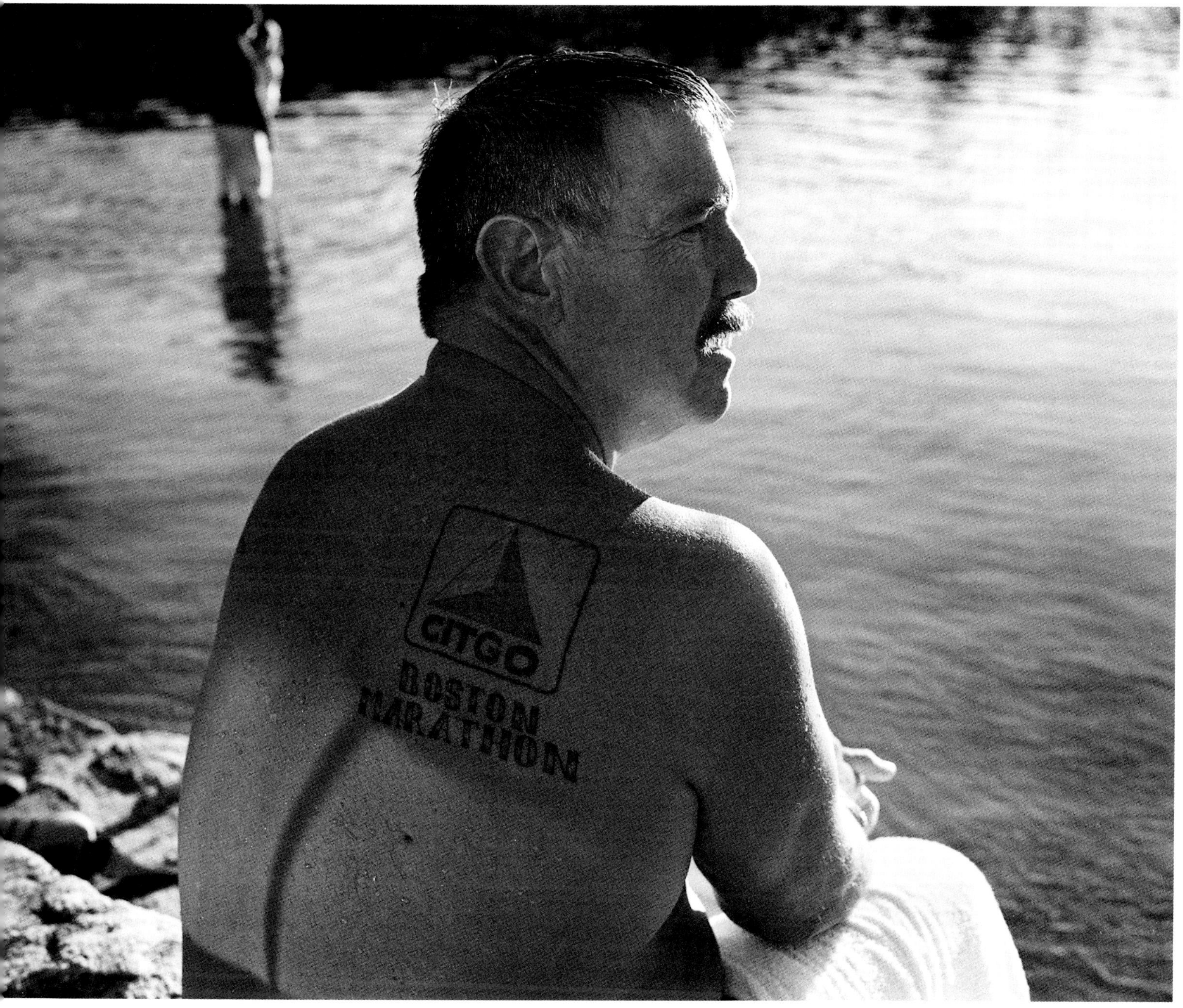
CITGO
BOSTON
MARATHON

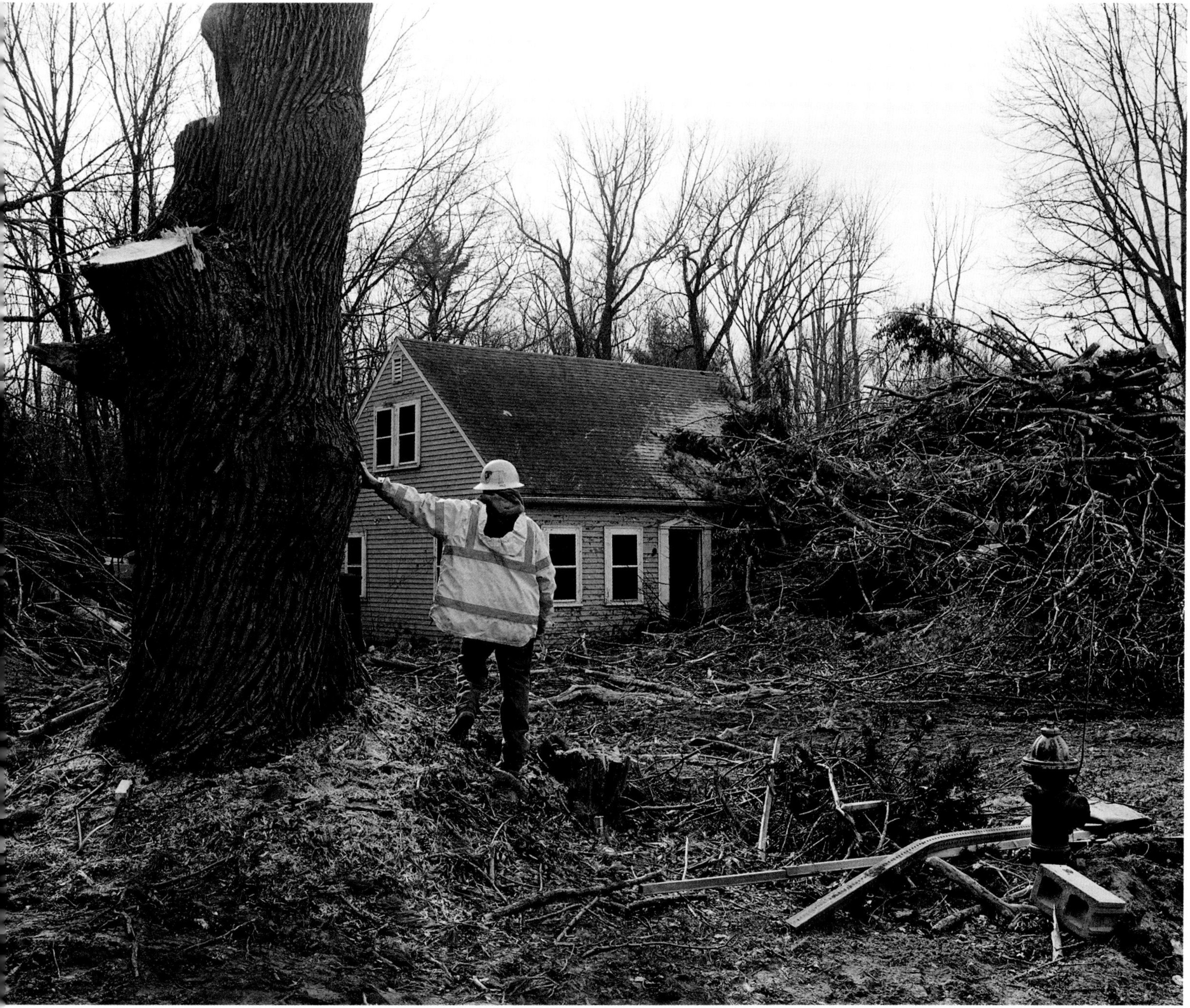

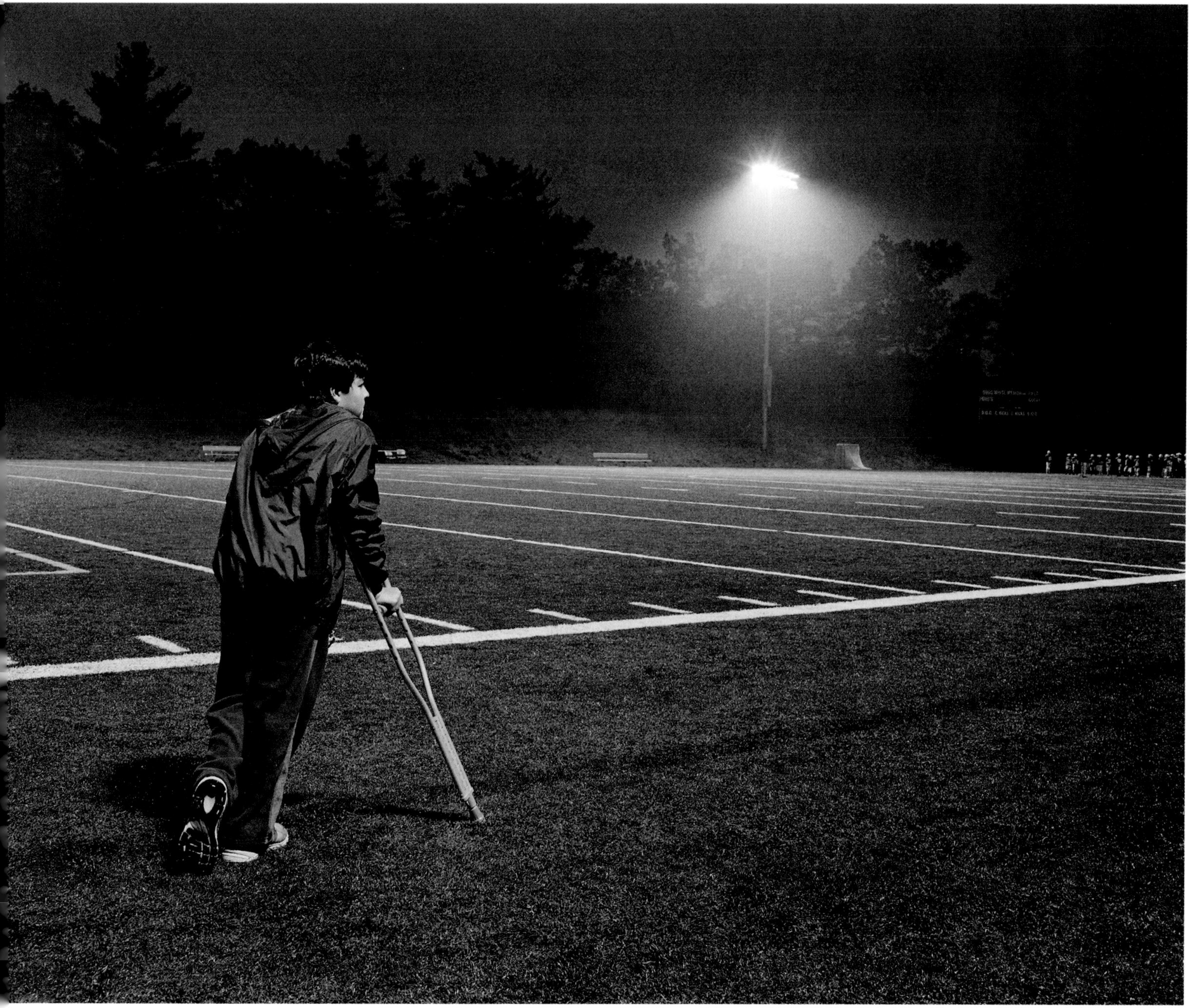

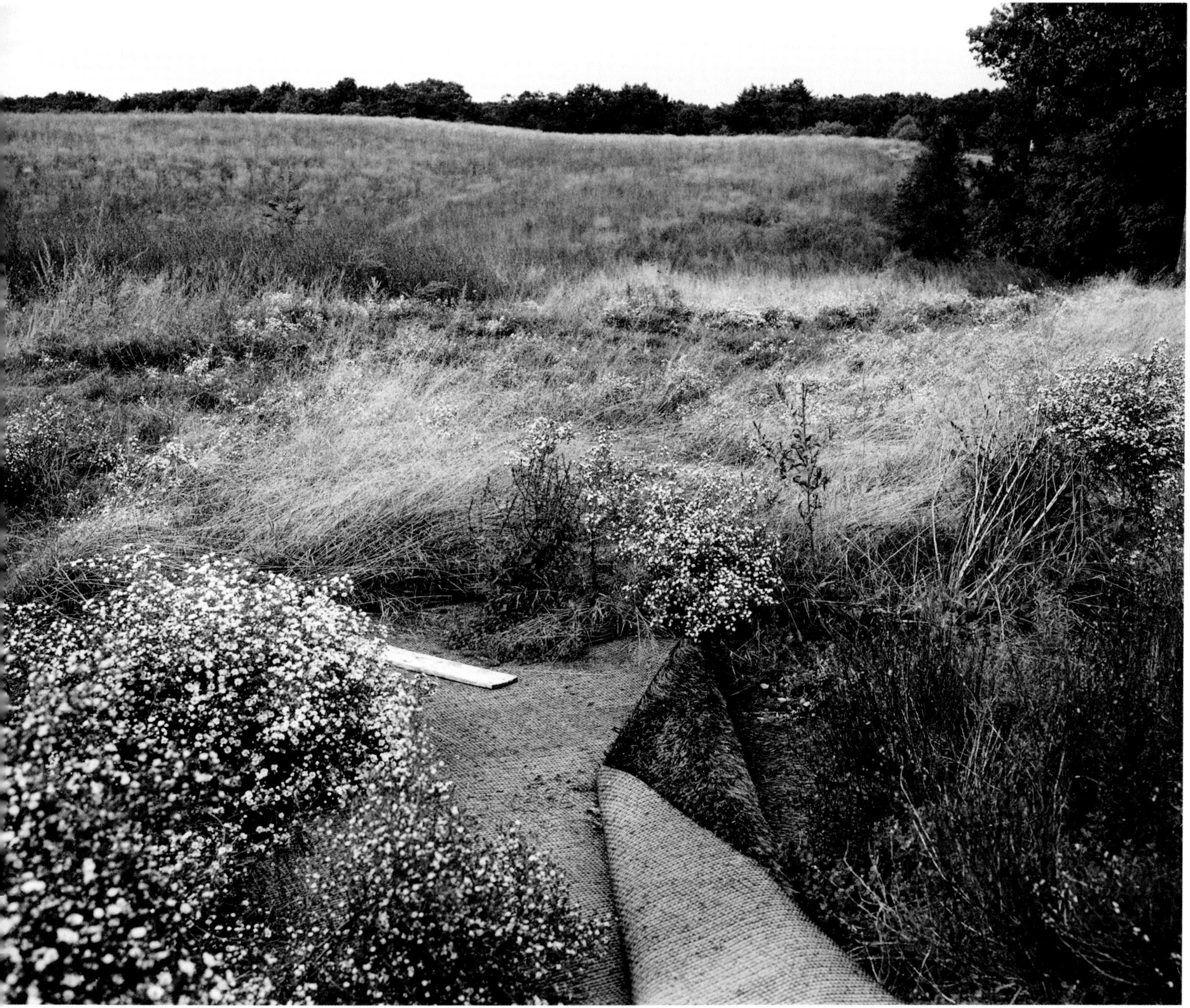

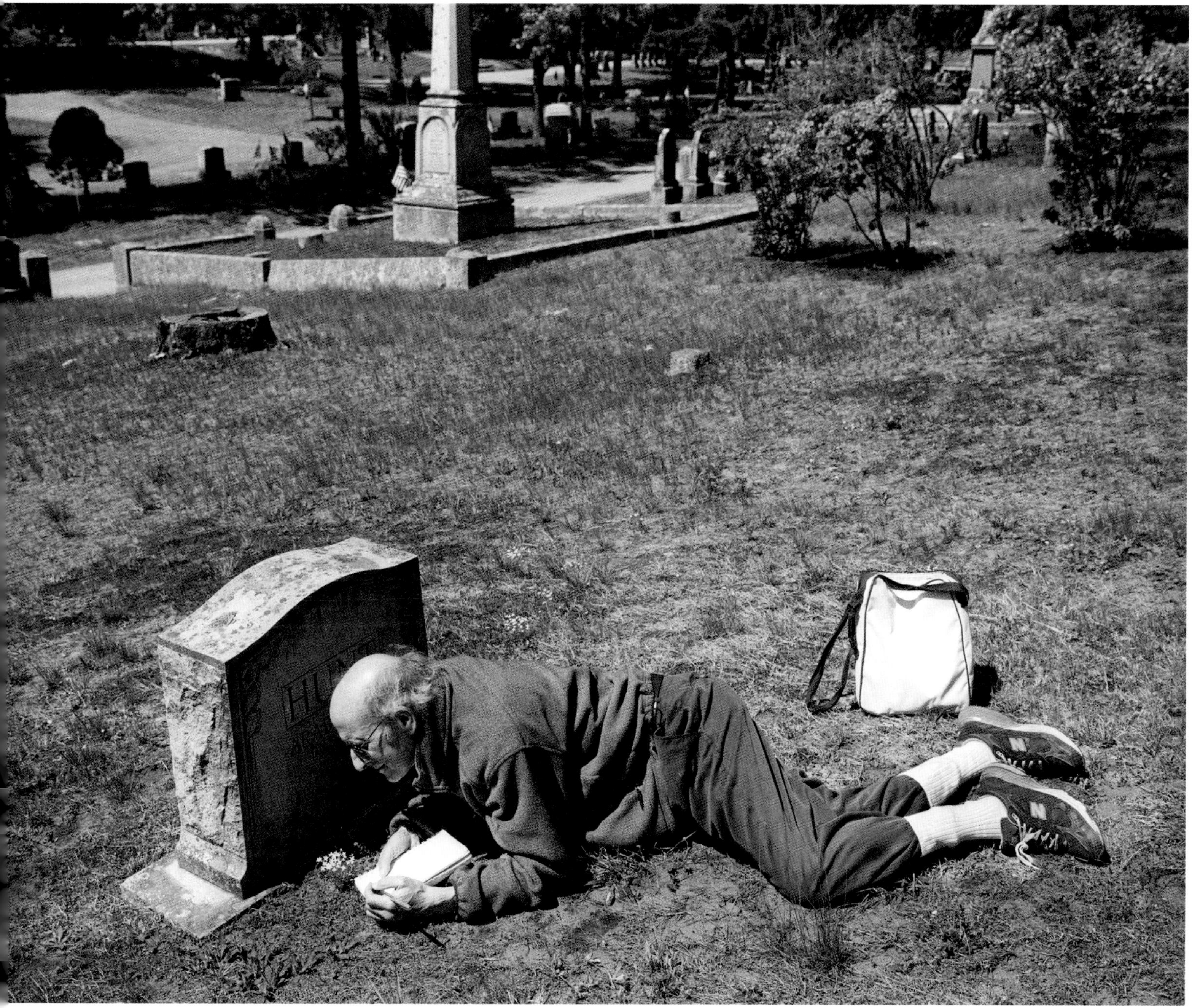

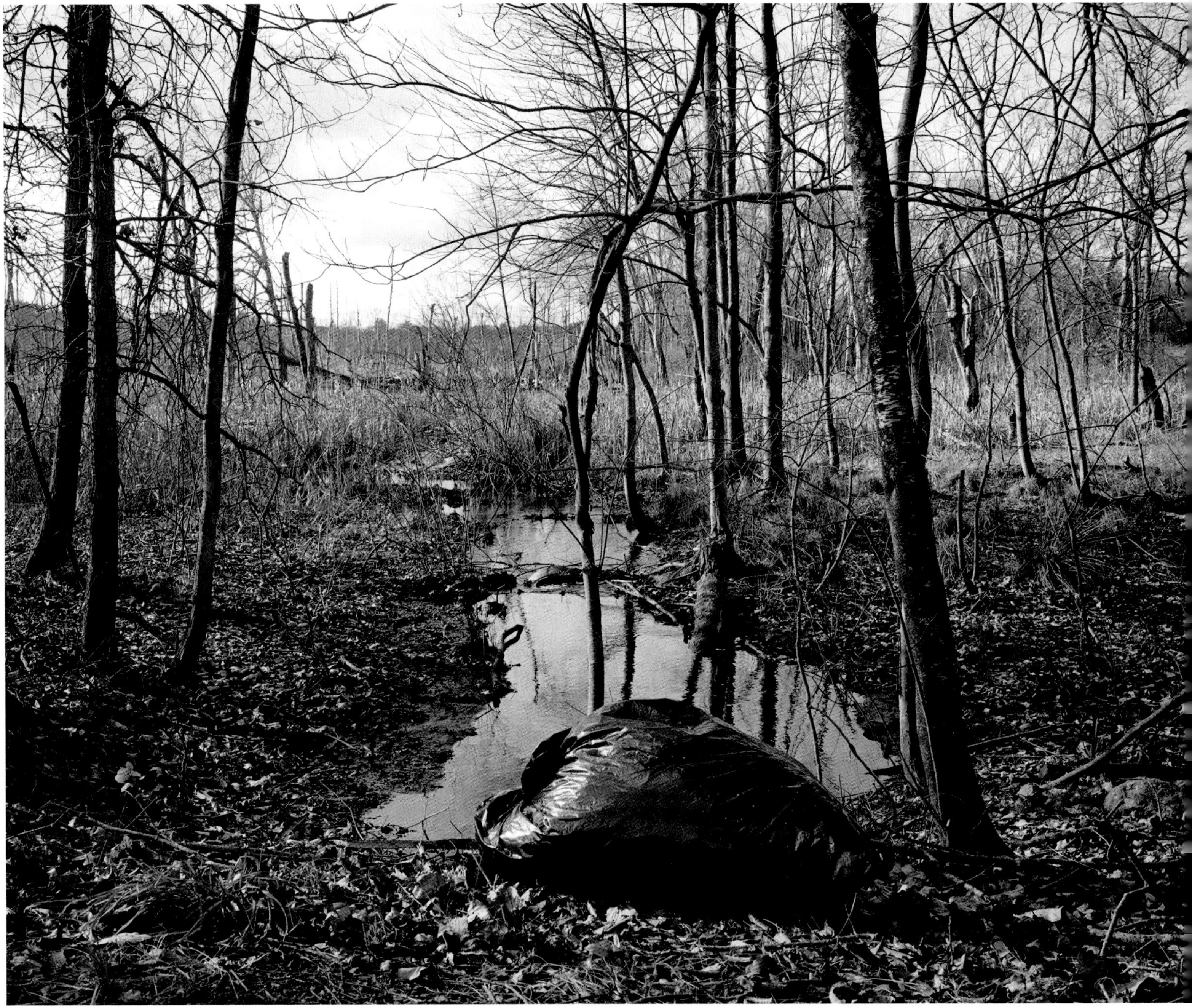

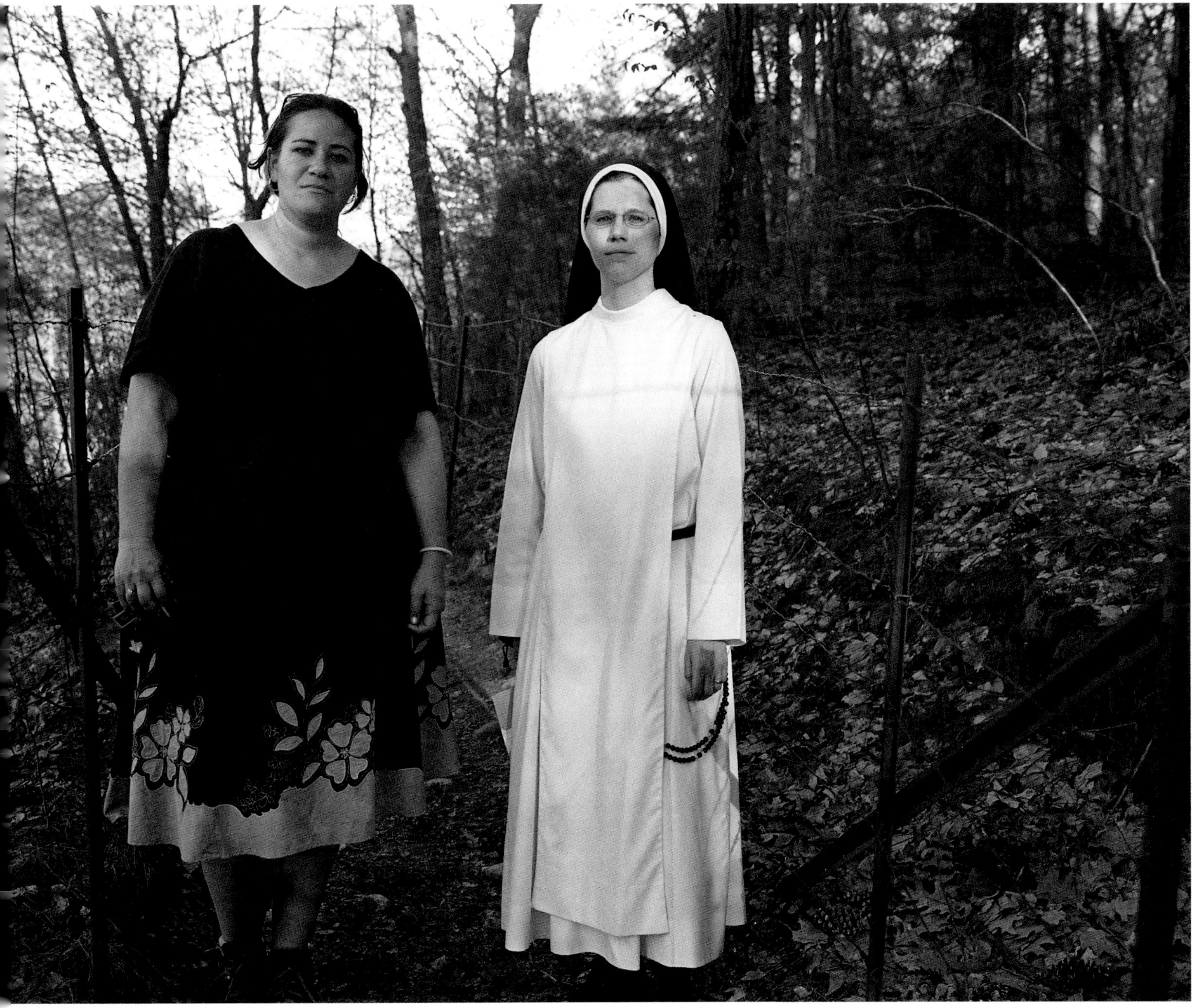

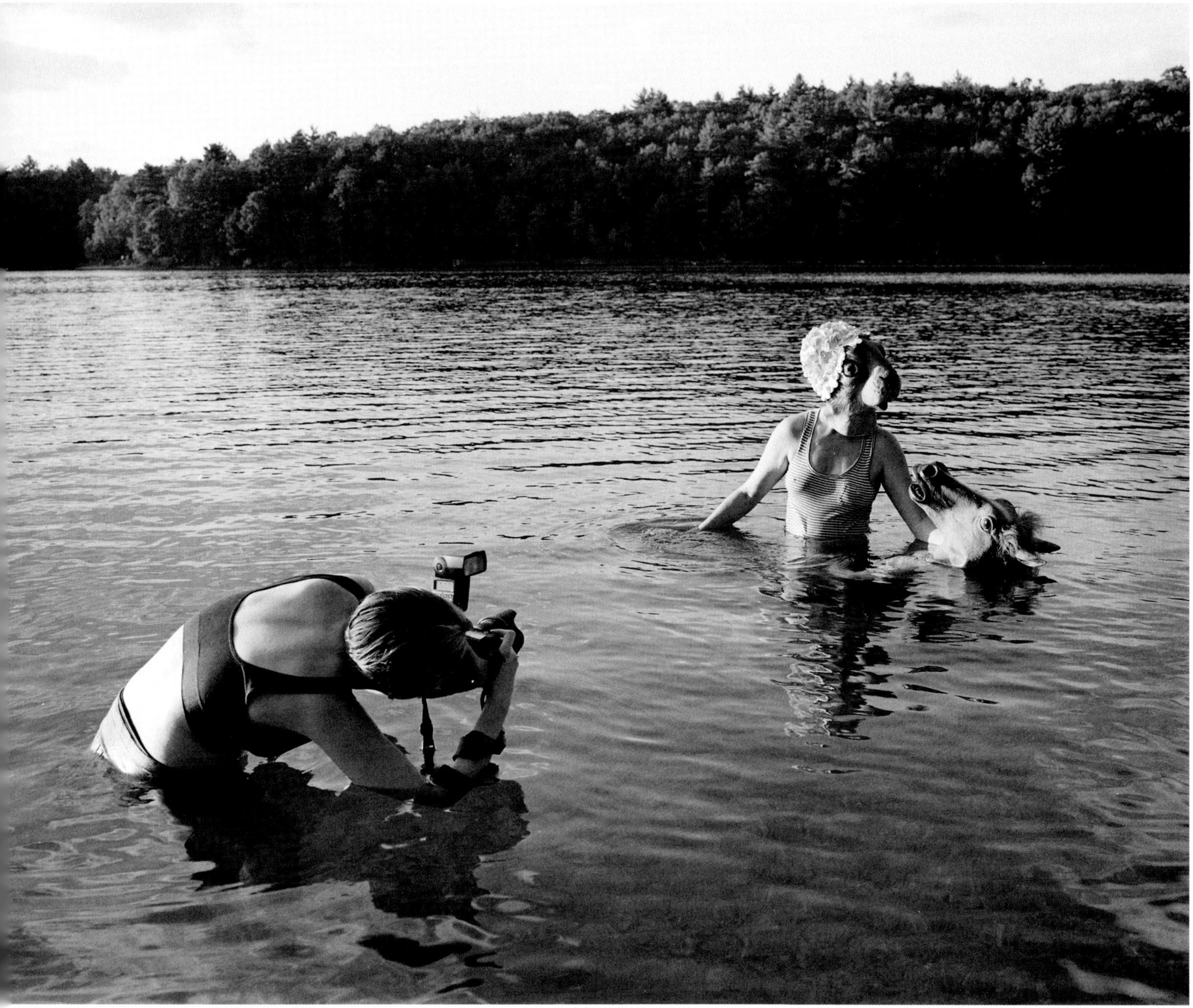

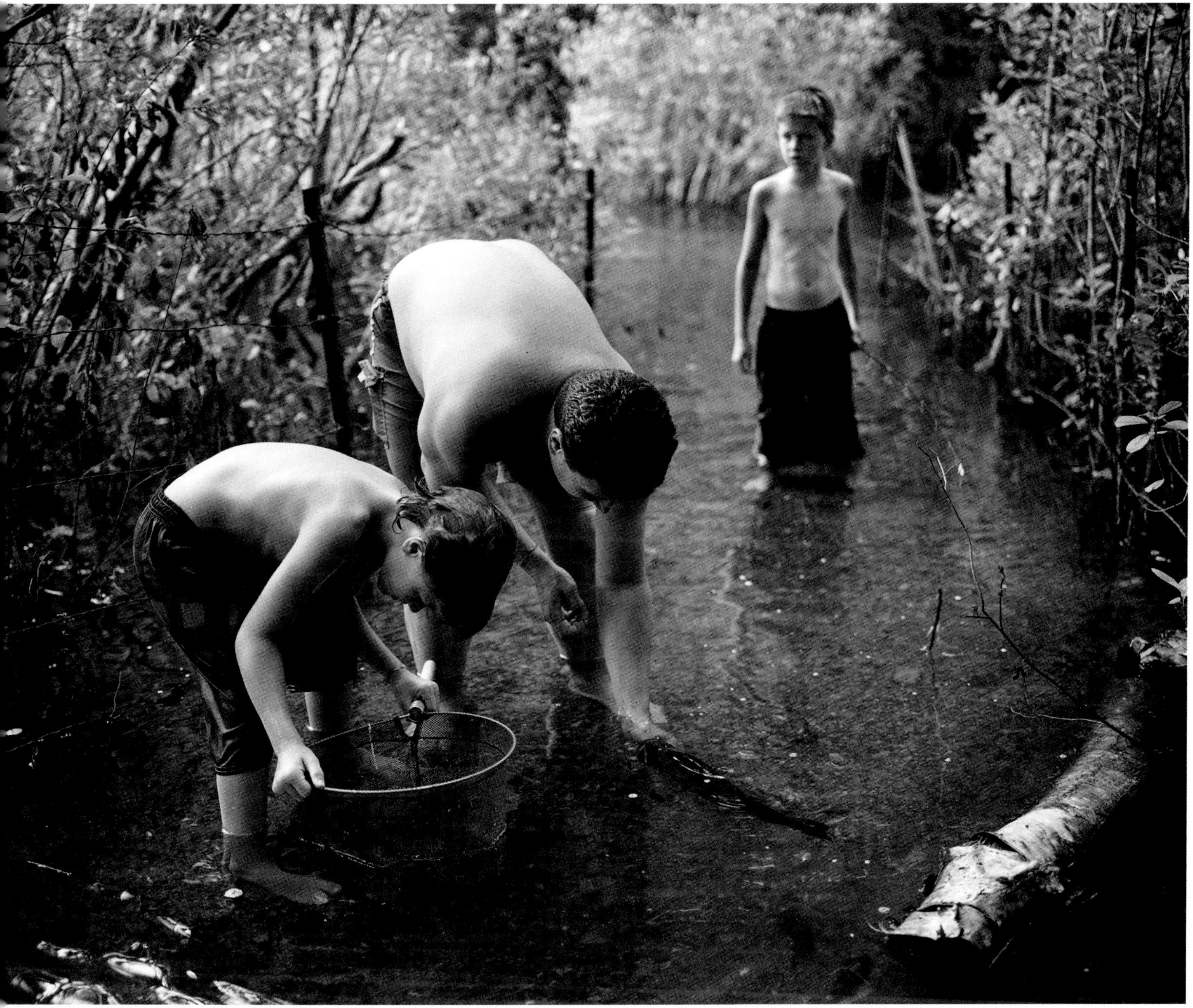

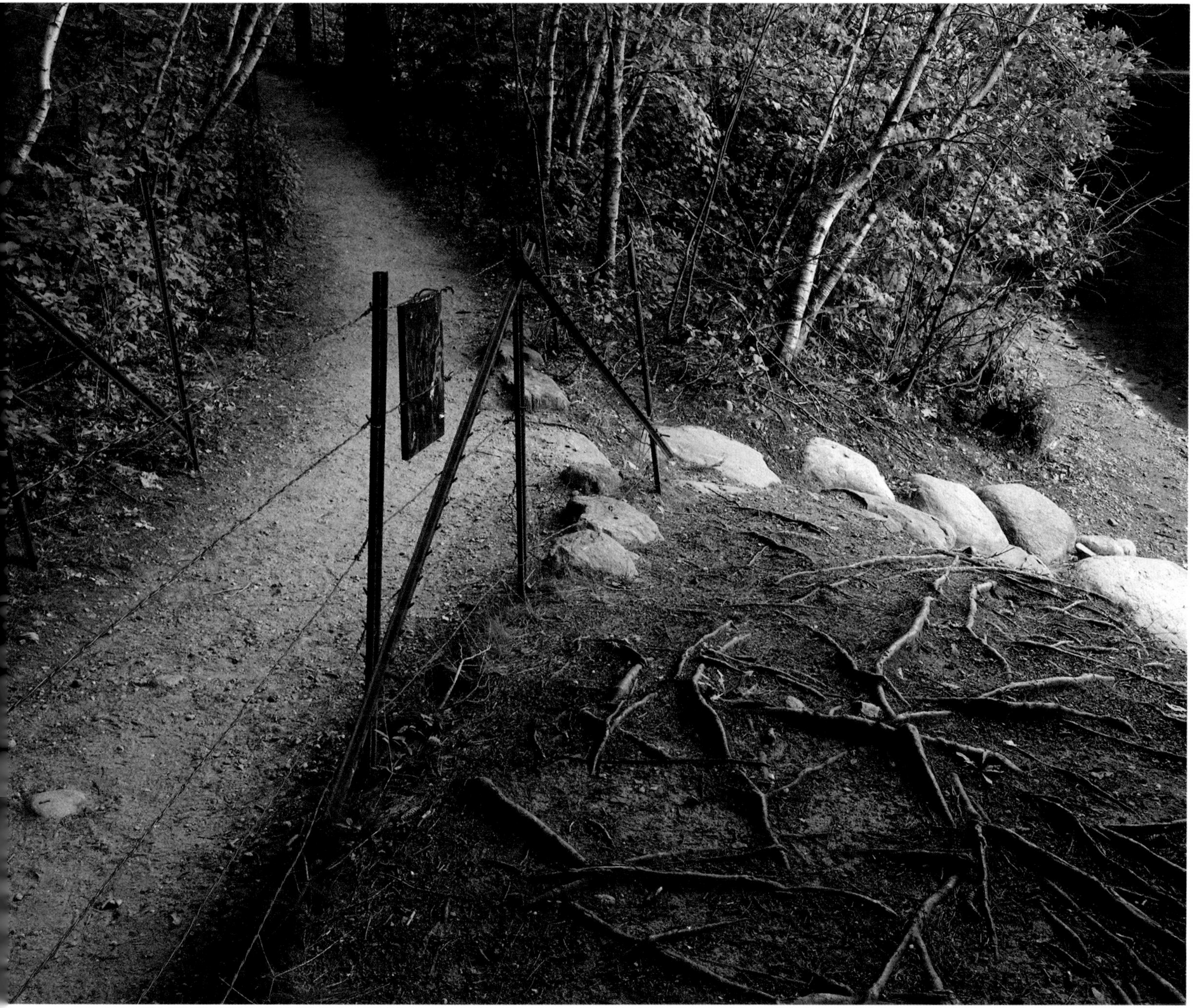

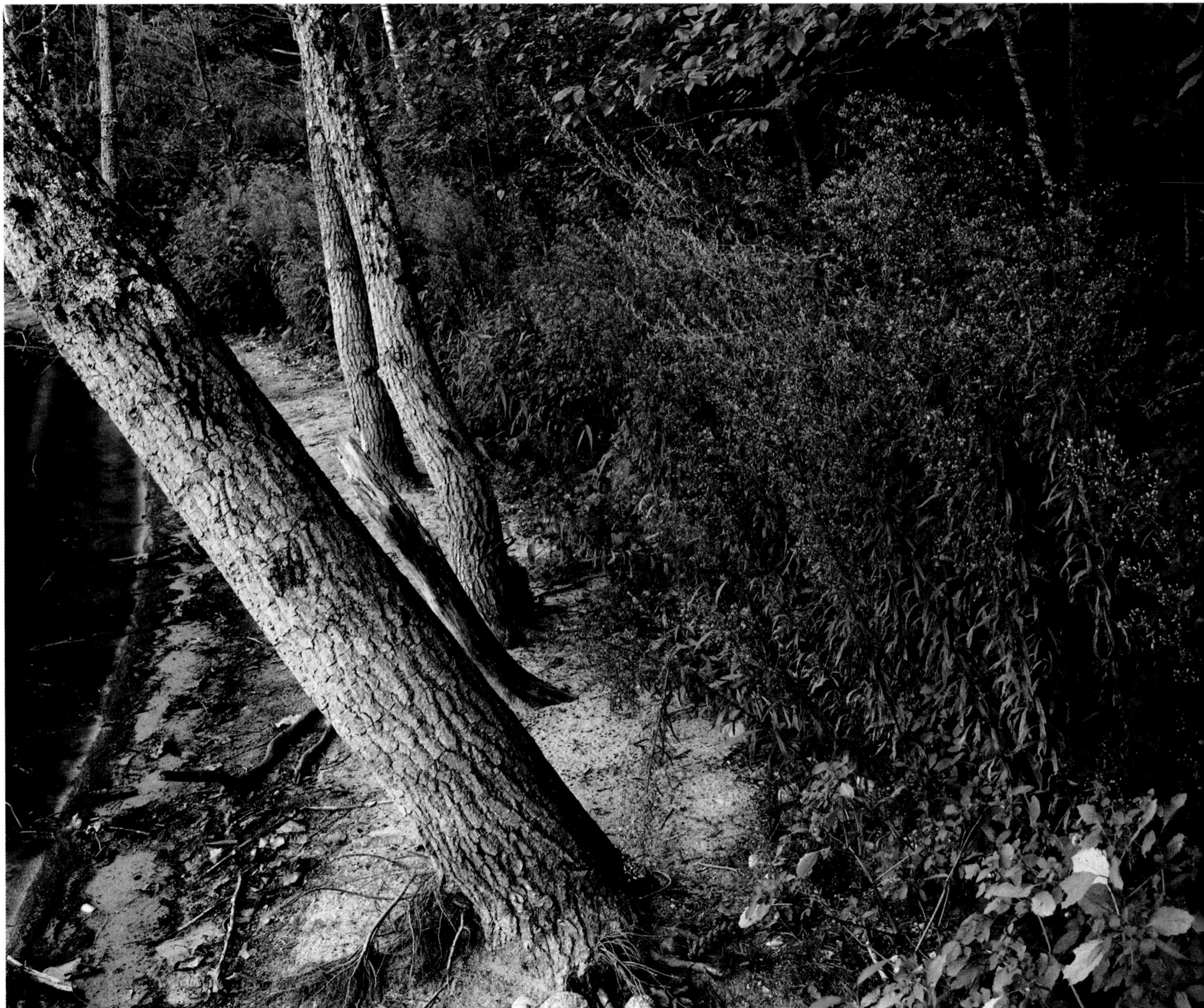

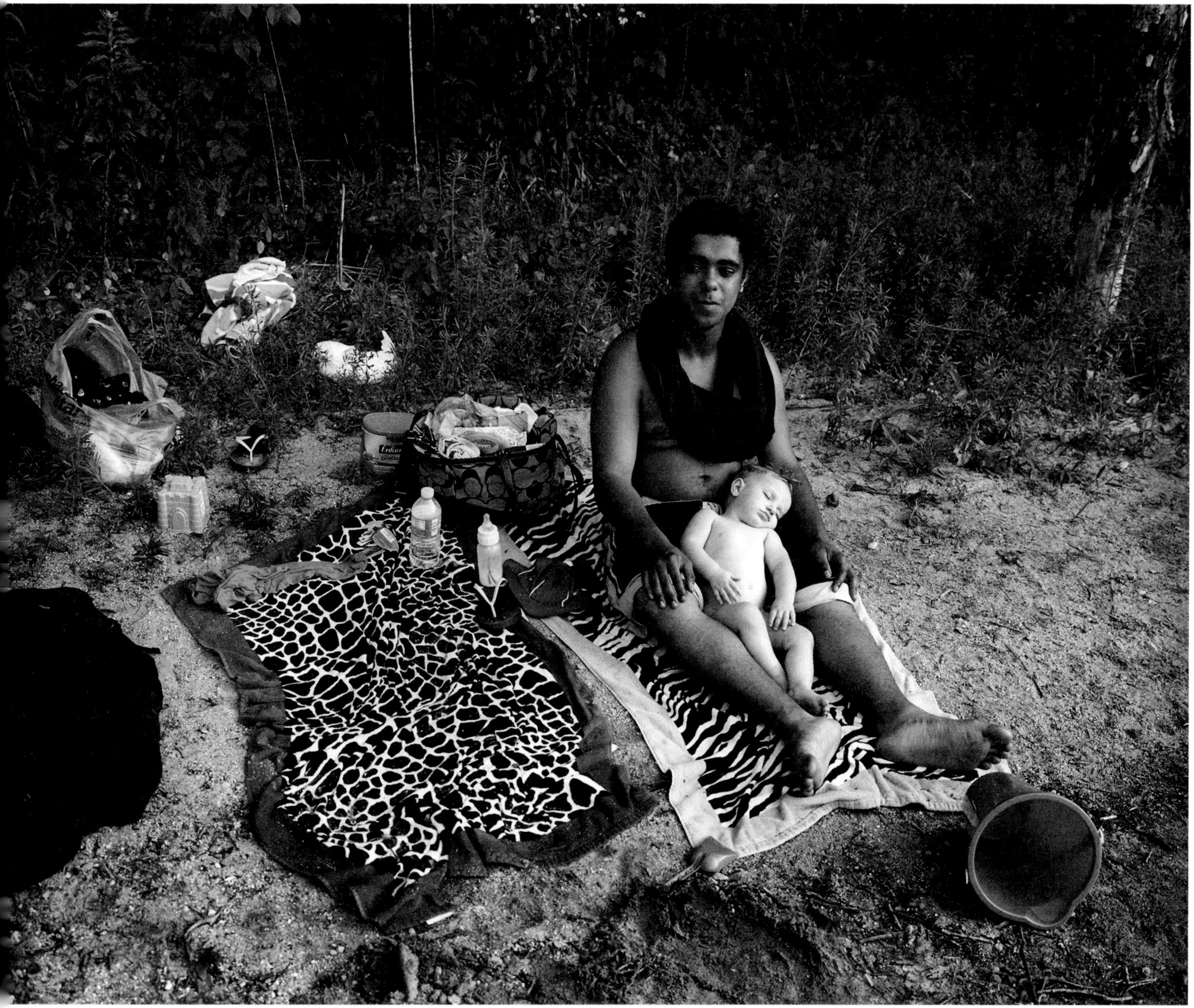

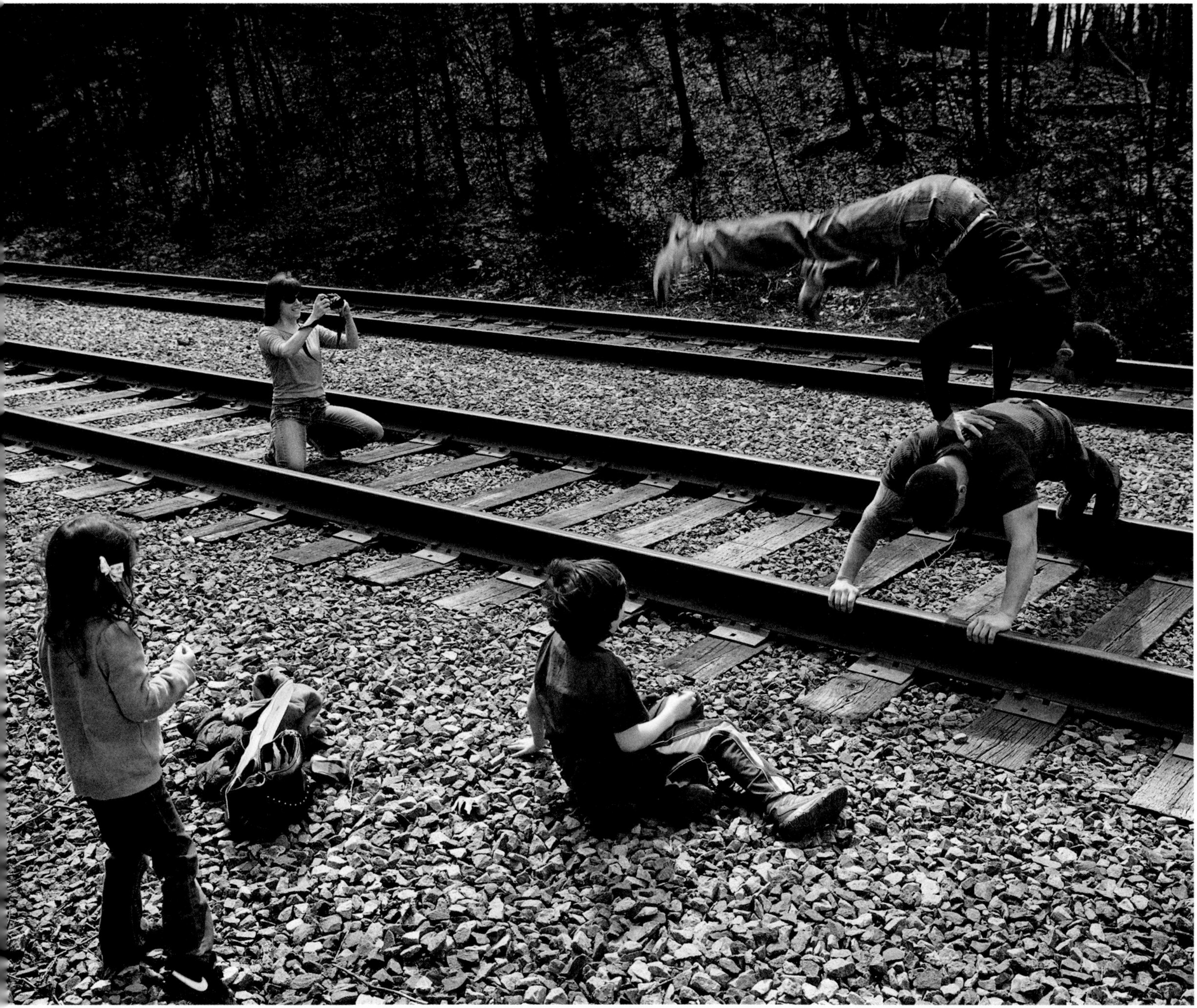

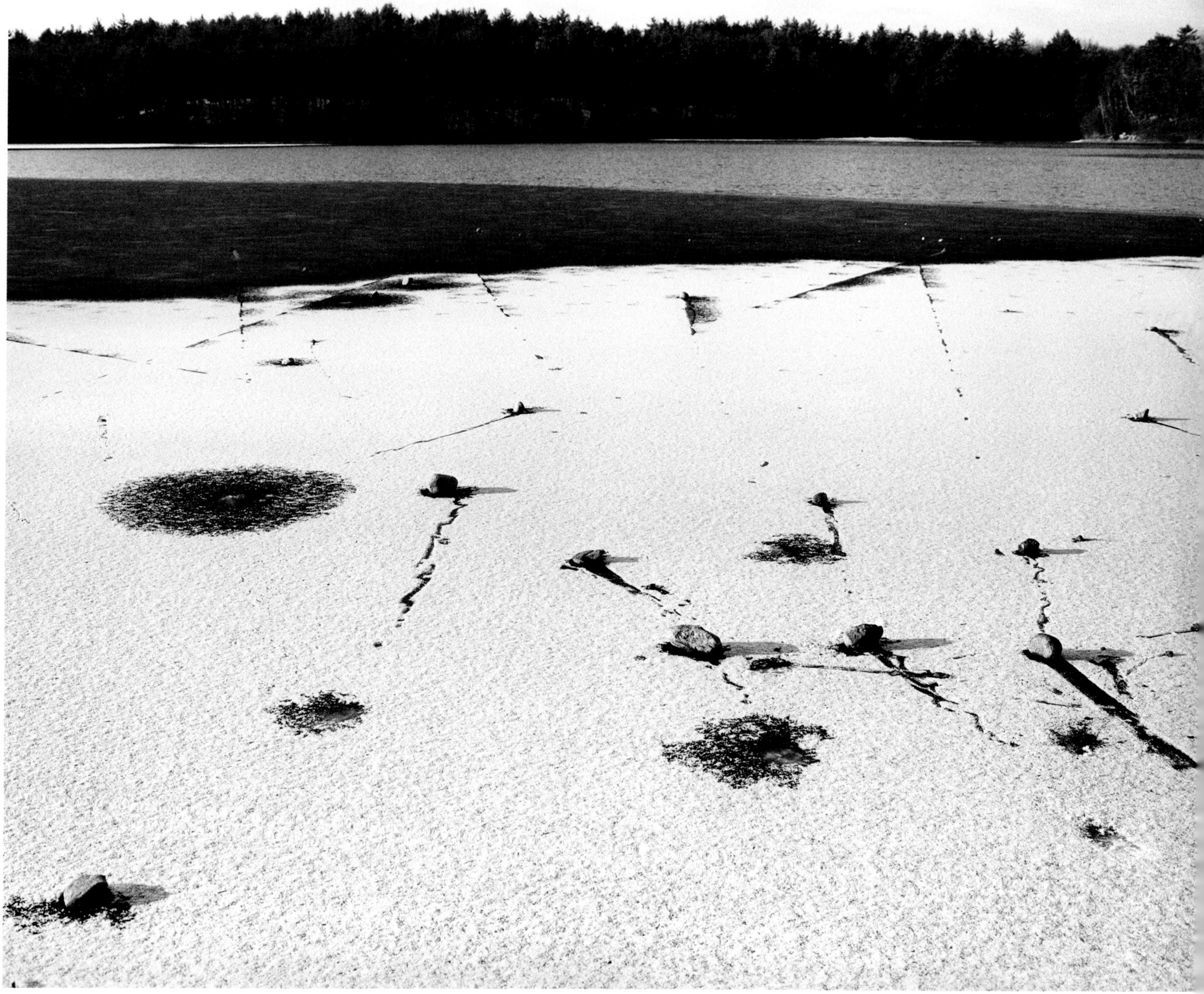

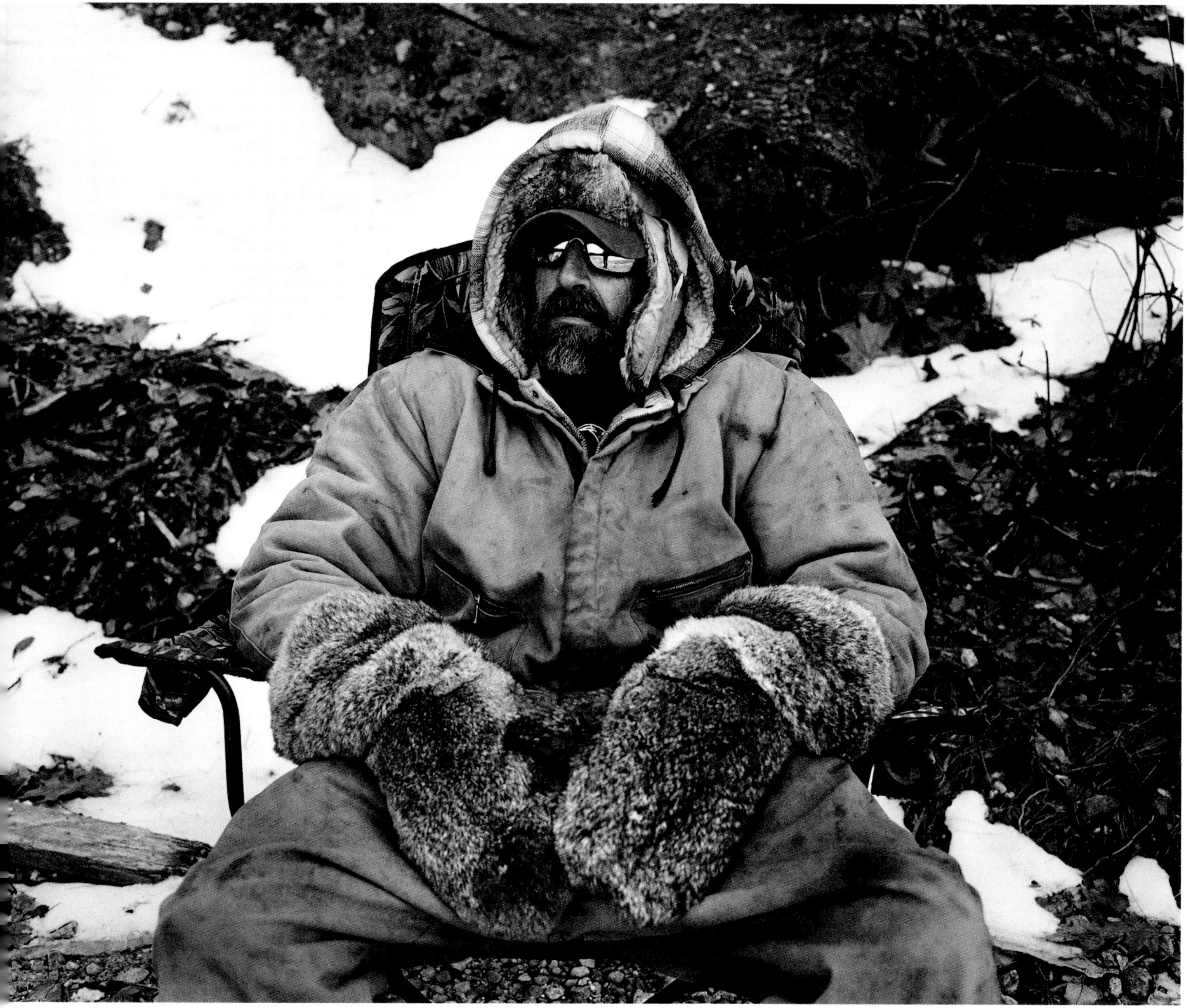

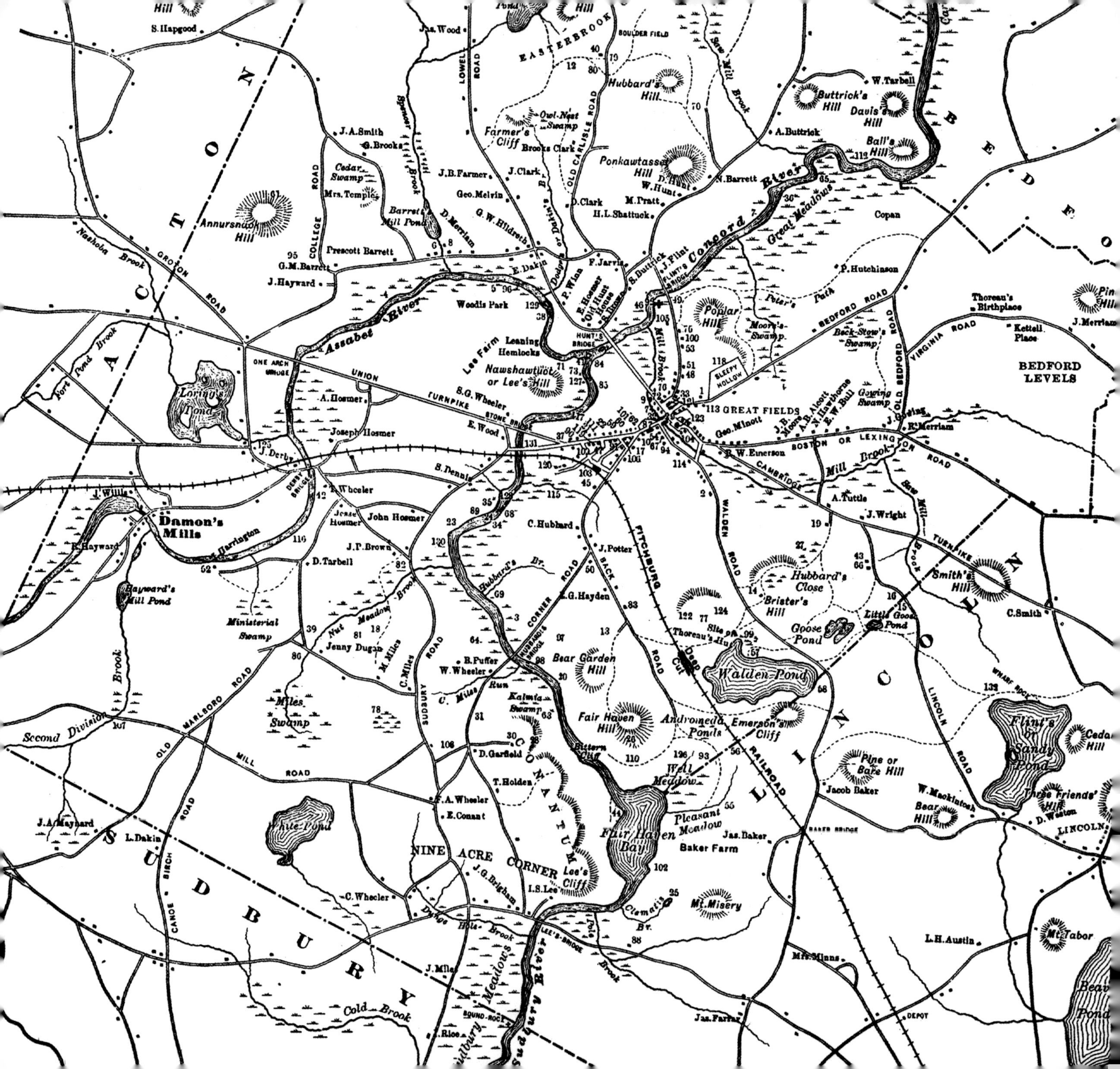

ACTON
BEDFORD
LINCOLN
SUDBURY
BEDFORD LEVELS
Concord River
Assabet River
Sudbury River
Sudbury Meadows
Great Meadows
Walden Pond
Fair Haven Bay
Flint's or Sandy Pond
White Pond
Loring's Pond
Goose Pond
Little Goose Pond
Hayward's Mill Pond
Barrett's Mill Pond
Annursnack Hill
Nawshawtuct or Lee's Hill
Ponkawtasset Hill
Hubbard's Hill
Buttrick's Hill
Davis's Hill
Ball's Hill
Poplar Hill
Brister's Hill
Bear Garden Hill
Fair Haven Hill
Emerson's Cliff
Pine or Bare Hill
Bear Hill
Smith's Hill
Three Friends' Hill
Mt. Misery
Mt. Tabor
Lee's Cliff
Bittern Cliff
Farmer's Cliff
CONANTUM
Owl-Nest Swamp
Cedar Swamp
Ministerial Swamp
Miles Swamp
Kalmia Swamp
Beck-Stow's Swamp
Moore's Swamp
Gowing Swamp
Andromeda Ponds
Well Meadow
Pleasant Meadow
Hubbard's Close
Site of Thoreau's Hut
Deep Cut
Damon's Mills
Baker Farm
NINE ACRE CORNER
GREAT FIELDS
SLEEPY HOLLOW
Thoreau's Birthplace
Kettell Place
Leaning Hemlocks
Lee Farm
Woodis Park
Copan
Peter's Path
Nashoba Brook
Fort Pond Brook
Spencer Brook
Saw Mill Brook
Mill Brook
Nut Meadow Brook
Hubbard's Br.
Second Division Brook
Dugan Hole Brook
Pole Brook
Clematis Br.
Cold Brook
C. Miles Run
Jenny Dugan
EASTERBROOK
BOULDER FIELD
LOWELL ROAD
OLD CARLISLE ROAD
COLLEGE ROAD
GROTON ROAD
UNION TURNPIKE
BEDFORD ROAD
OLD BEDFORD ROAD
VIRGINIA ROAD
BOSTON OR LEXINGTON ROAD
CAMBRIDGE TURNPIKE
WALDEN ROAD
LINCOLN ROAD
CORNER ROAD
SUDBURY ROAD
OLD MARLBORO ROAD
MILL ROAD
CANOE BIRCH ROAD
FITCHBURG RAILROAD
BACK ROAD
WHARF ROCK
ONE ARCH BRIDGE
STONE BRIDGE
DERBY BRIDGE
HUNT'S BRIDGE
FLINT'S BRIDGE
HUBBARD'S BRIDGE
BAKER BRIDGE
LEE'S BRIDGE
BOUND-ROCK
DEPOT
LINCOLN
R. W. Emerson

Two Waldens

"In Walden Thoreau is clear, as Emerson seldom was, about the location of meaning and value. He says that it does not reside in the natural facts or in the social institutions or in anything 'out there,' but in the consciousness. It is a product of imaginative perception, of the analogy-perceiving, metaphor-making, mythopoeic power of the human mind."

Leo Marx

Walden, the title of S.B. Walker's book, points to a place, in the broad sense of that word, a small uneven oval of water near similar ponds and three rivers, a location in a landscape. But of course this is no common place; it is a place like no other. Its fame and significance rest not on anything of historical importance that happened there but entirely on a work of literature; an extended essay that recounts observations of nature, storytelling and history, narrative and philosophical analysis. The title, in short, serves more purposes than topographical.

The landscape surveyed by Walker and his camera was once home to another surveyor of sorts, the American writer Henry David Thoreau. There, at the age of 28, he famously retreated to a one room cabin by the pond for two years, to live simply and record his thoughts and feelings, put down in a series of journal entries out which he would eventually craft the book for which he is most often remembered; *Walden*. Over the course of Thoreau's book, the word 'Walden' assumes larger, wider, more complex and challenging meanings. It becomes the name of a philosophical (and aesthetic) stance, an outlook, a perspective, a way of looking and being in the world. Because the 19th century writer explains and articulates Walden as place and idea at once, he transforms the word Walden into the name not just of a distinct place but into a way of being, of being there, of living in the imagination of a single and singular place, of living in full self-consciousness of that fact, that being alive in Walden means necessarily being alive in and for oneself.

S.B. Walker's borrowed title, then, invests his work with the significance of a philosophical undertaking, from the pictures themselves to how he presents them. Through the seasons and changing weather, he takes us on a peripatetic journey into Thoreau country. From the edge of the pond to a nearby landfill, through parking lots and swamps, down winding forest paths and train tracks, we travel a formerly pastoral landscape that has slipped into the realm of the suburban. Like Thoreau, he points to contemporary society and its temporal inflections, yet does so in ways that remind us of the deeply mysterious nature of being. We see images of people on cell phones wearing styles of clothing which someday soon will appear dated, punctuated with close-ups of water and ice that suggest the unchanging qualities of the infinite. Walker set his sights on the transcendent possibilities of the here and now. In looking for an all-embracing theme, we return to the title and its tantalizing implications. "Walden" cannot help but bring to mind simultaneously a place on a map and a book, an object held in the hand for the sake of the reading experience and the text it communicates. Can we say that Walker's book is analogous to the pond in that the landscape and its denizens, like the book, are something to be read in a manner similar to the way we read the book by Thoreau?

Though Walker's "Walden" should not be taken as a direct reading or interpretation of Thoreau's great book, that book and its author are very definitely within the realm of the photographs. We can say that Walker's book hinges upon Thoreau's vision in a most fundamental regard. Thoreau tells the story of his stay at Walden Pond as an experiment in how to live, a story of "where I lived and what I lived for." He tells it as a story of America itself, a story of independence (indeed, his book has been described as a second American Declaration of Independence), of going into "nature" to discover how an independent life can be lived. His Walden Pond is a place of still, pristine waters and natural processes of seasonal change, of blossoming and dying, of regeneration into new life.

Walker's pictures, on the other hand, show something gone seriously wrong at this cherished site, a monument to American idealism and a belief in ever-recurring rebirth and transformation. The essence of Thoreau's optimistic American vision of the redemptive powers of nature appears in the rapturous description of the melting of winter snow and the coming of spring in fresh growth witnessed everywhere in the woods. Walker's purpose is not to exalt natural process but to view nature –the waters of the pond, the trails, trees, and vegetation that mark the shoreline– as reminders of a time when this very place gave rise to Thoreau's vision of American possibility. American industrialization was in its very early stages when Thoreau lived and wrote his Walden, the sounds of the railroad an ominous note in his story but not one yet fatal to his encompassing vision. By contrast, Walker's Walden Pond seems already overcome by the destructive forces of modern life.

In the opening picture the telling sign of decisive change from Thoreau's experience are the words "Walden Patrol" emblazoned on the outboard motorboat churning the now restless waters of the pond. It has become a place requiring policing. Throughout the book we see wire fences, the worn out paths of legions of beach-goers, and the tell-tale marks of chain saws, further signs of how decisively Walker's vision diverges from Thoreau's. Because Walker's vision is embodied in photographs, it is grounded in visual fact. His vision derives from the way things are, the changes that have occurred since Thoreau, confirmed by the camera. A note of pathos wends through the pictures; we sense it especially in the absence of signs of human pleasure, of well-being along with the more compelling signs of damaged human bodies and emotions.

This seems a frozen Walden, a freeze too deep to be redeemed by first aid alone. Walker carries his Thoreau along with his camera, and by claiming "Walden" for his title, he offers Thoreau –and through him the entire tradition of American romanticism– a formative role in his own extraordinary book. Walker's pictures are layered against each other to reveal an unrelenting vision of disenchantment with what Walden Pond once represented to enthralled Americans.

Two images give particular force to this notion of declension in American beliefs: the biologist spread prone on the ground next to a gravestone, gathering a record of flowering times as evidence of climate change and its fatal implications for Thoreau's hopeful view of the ever-recurring rebirth of nature, and the final image of the ice melt, which in the original Walden gave rise to a rapturous account of the regenerative process of the natural world. Here the melt frees the waters only to reveal, floating helpless on the liberated waters, a shopping bag stamped with the logo of the department store chain Target, the final irony in the joining of the two Waldens. That sad and saddening image culminates the nourishing role that Thoreau and his book play in shaping and deepening S.B. Walker's vision, a vision of the continuing creative presence of American romanticism in defining reality in contemporary America.

Alan Trachtenberg
Neil Gray, Jr. Professor Emeritus of
English and American Studies,
Yale University

NOTES

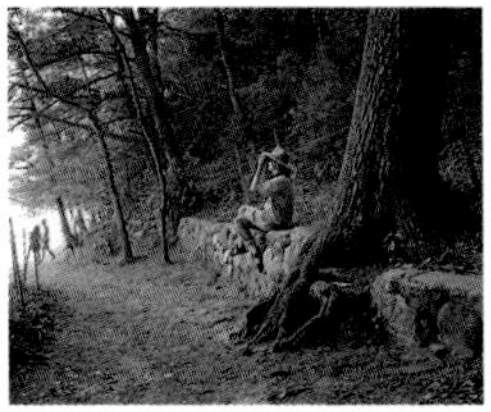

Frontispiece:
Mike, birdwatching,
July 2011.

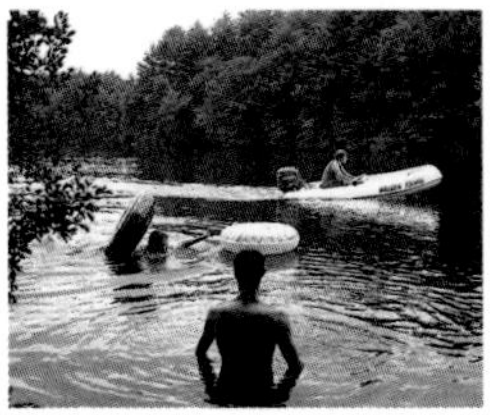

1 Walden Patrol,
July 2010.

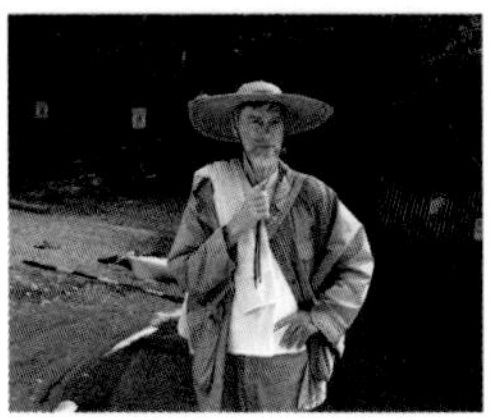

2 Win, one of the
regulars,
June 2010.

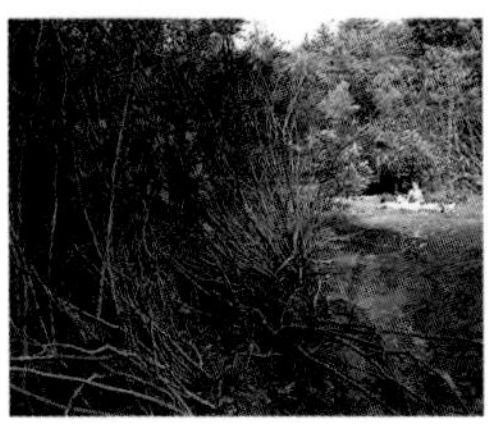

3 Thoreau's Cove,
three graces,
August 2011.

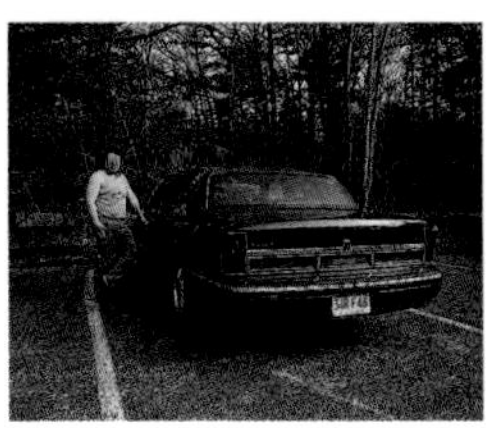

4 Bob and his
Lincoln,
May 2011.

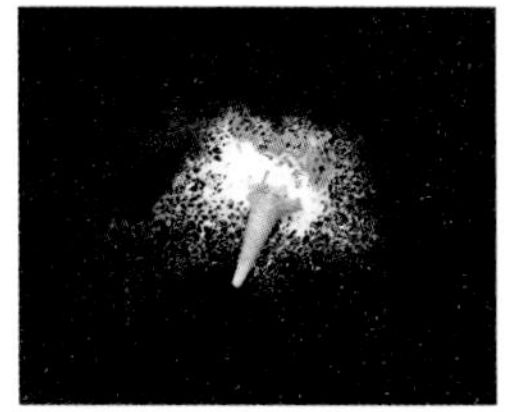

5 The Milky Way,
October 2010.

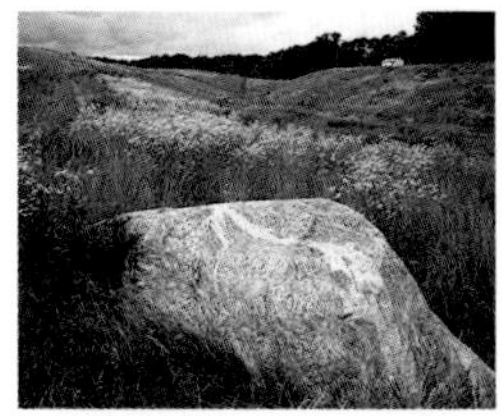

6 The Concord landfill,
1200 feet from the
edge of Walden Pond,
July 2012.

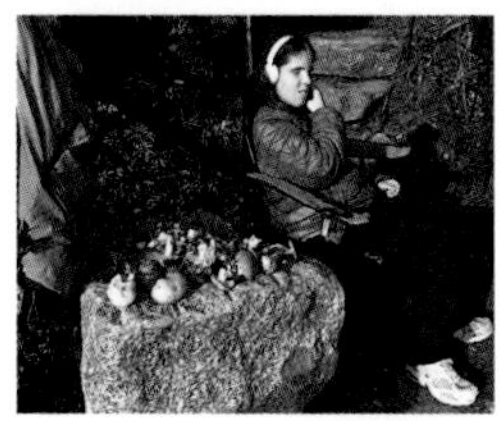

7 Lily, blind, sitting near
mushrooms,
October 2012.

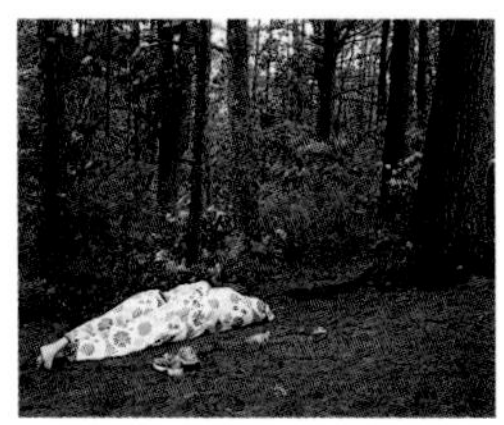

8 Storm approaching,
couple taking cover,
June 2012.

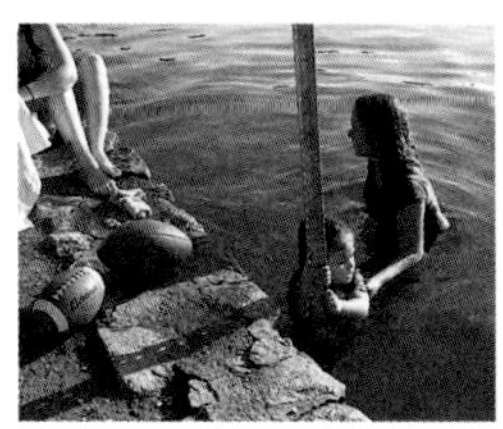

9 Girl clinging
to sign post, high
water.
August 2010.

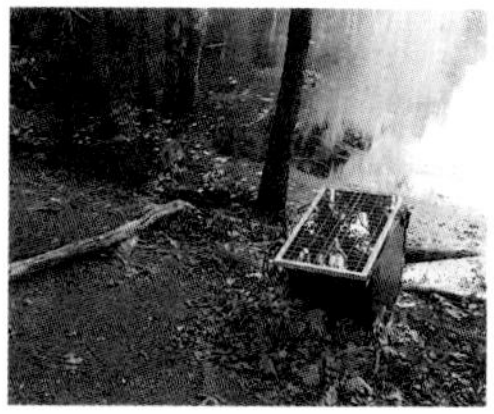

10 Solar collector / Alex MacLean's time-lapse camera, June 2010.

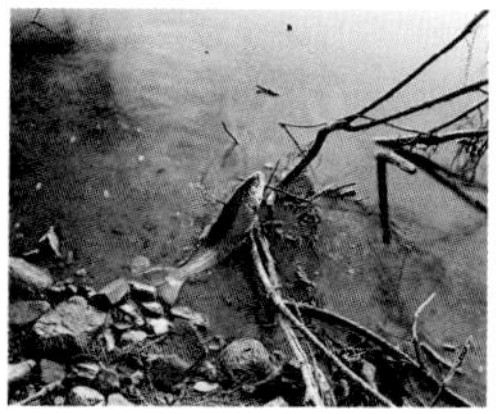

11 Trout, pond stocked by the state, July 2011.

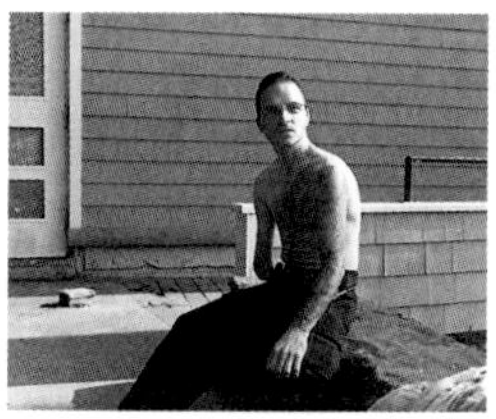

12 One-armed camp counseler from Revere, July 2010.

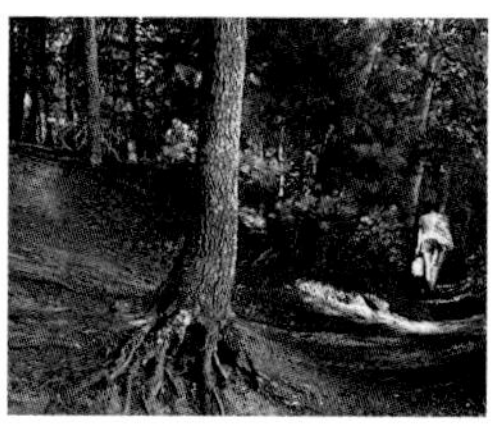

13 Tree near Thoreau's house site, September 2011.

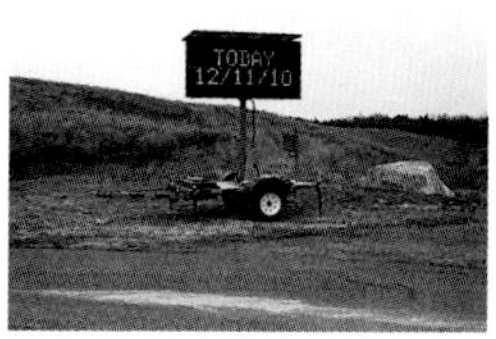

14 TODAY, Concord landfill, December 2010.

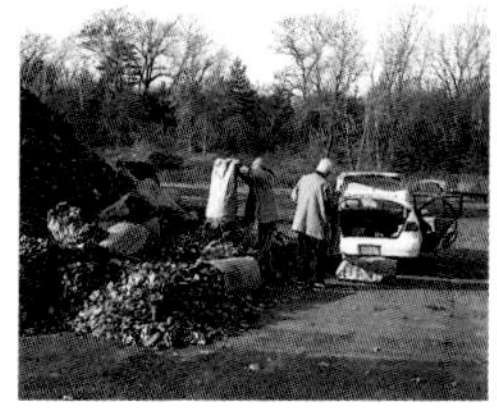

15 Leaf Day at the Concord landfill, November 2010.

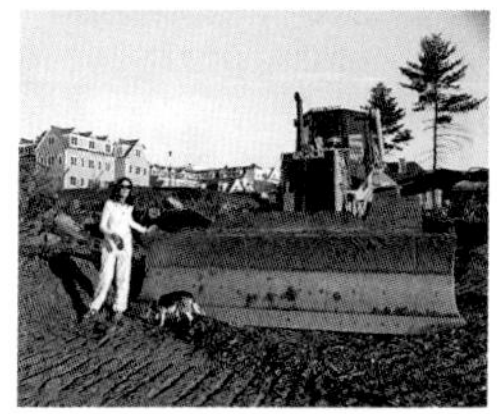

16 Rt. 2 Expansion, woman with bulldozer, April 2013.

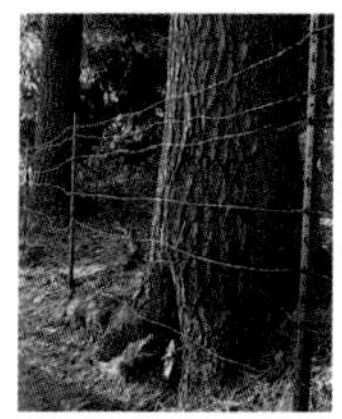

17 Fenced in path around Walden, November 2011.

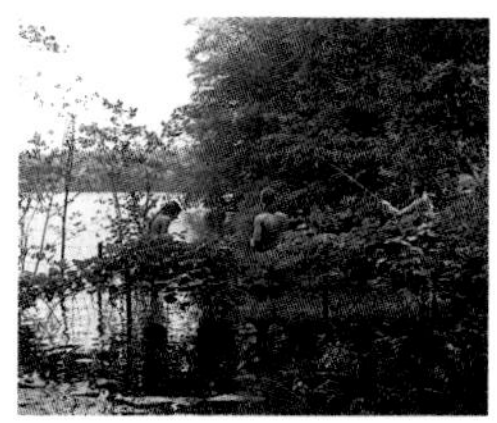

18 Teens fishing on a flooded path, July 2010.

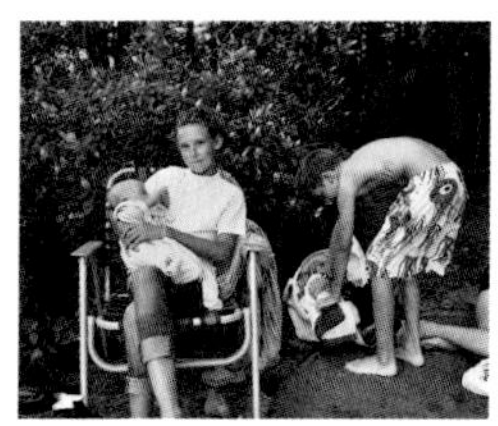

19 Mothering, August 2011.

20 Black Ice on the Pond, January 2011.

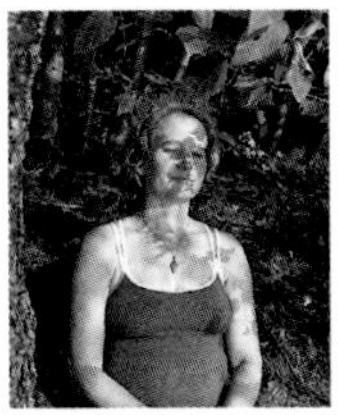

21 Woman, Shadow, July 2011.

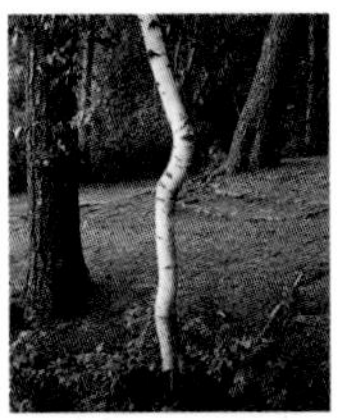

22 Birch, June 2012.

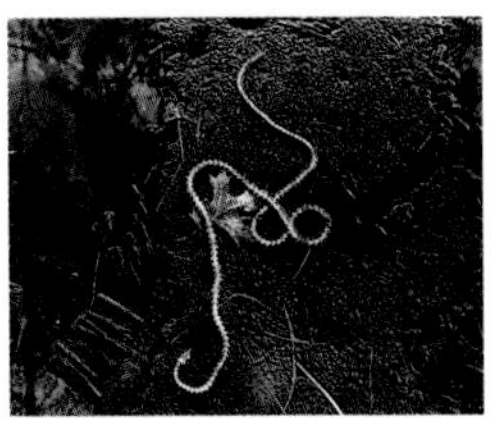

23 Snake skeleton at ice-out, March 2011.

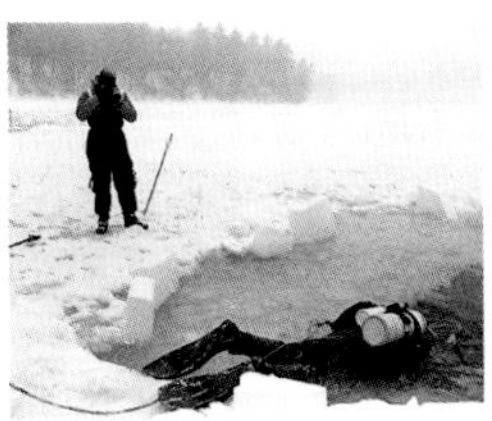

24 Massachusetts State Trooper underwater recovery training, Februrary 2014.

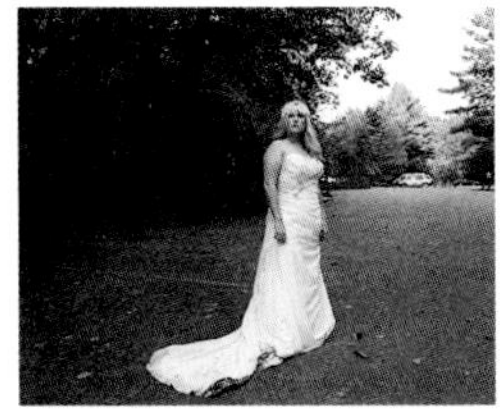

25 Bride at the beach parking lot after a swim in her dress, October 2011.

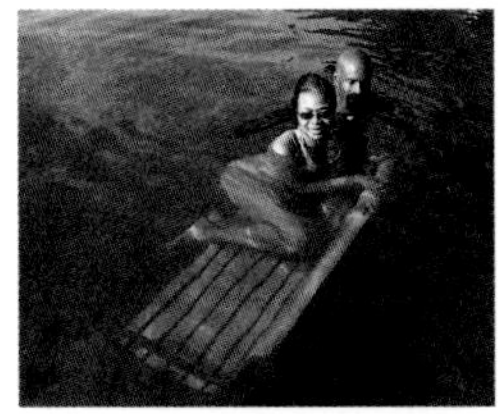

26 Submerged park bench, high-water, bathers, August 2010.

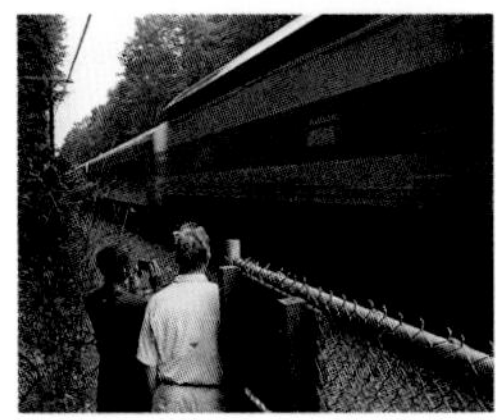

27 The Fitchburg railroad, 40 ft. from ponds edge, onlookers, August 2012.

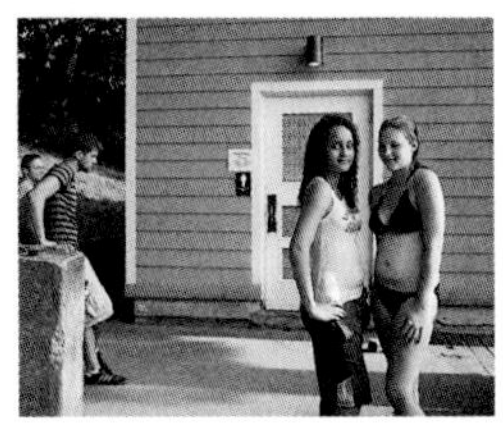

28 Girls posing by the bath house, July 2010.

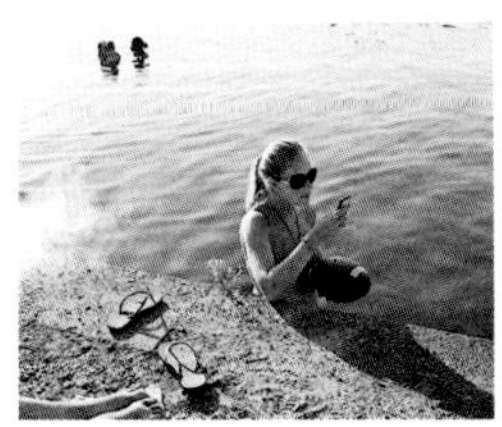

29 Phone, Football, Smoke, July 2010.

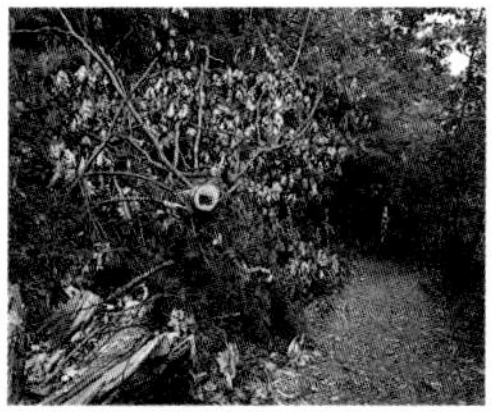

30 Fallen tree,
distant figure,
June 2011.

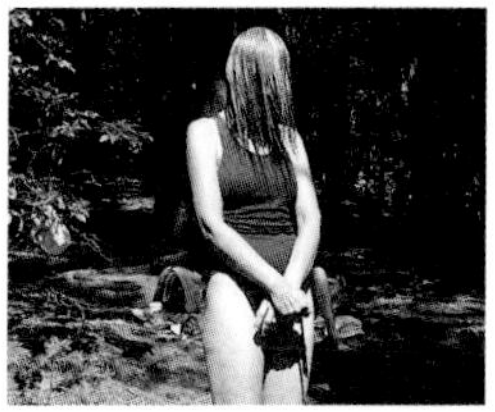

31 Combing hair
after a swim,
August 2010.

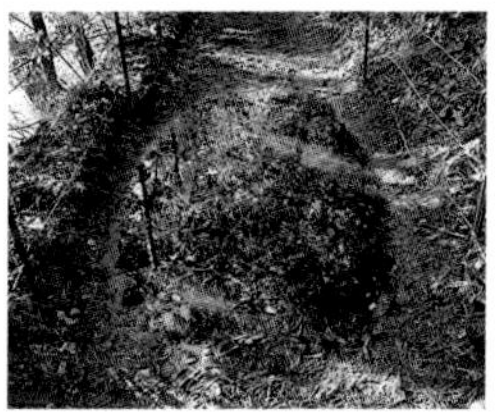

32 Puddle,
November 2011.

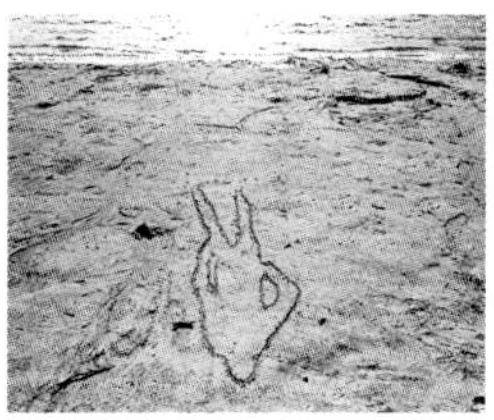

33 Shadow tracing,
April 2012.

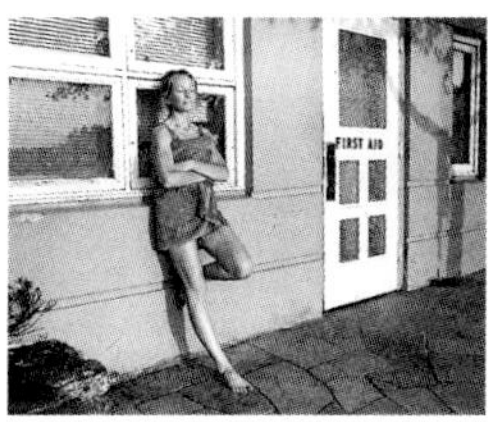

34 Swimmer,
September 2012.

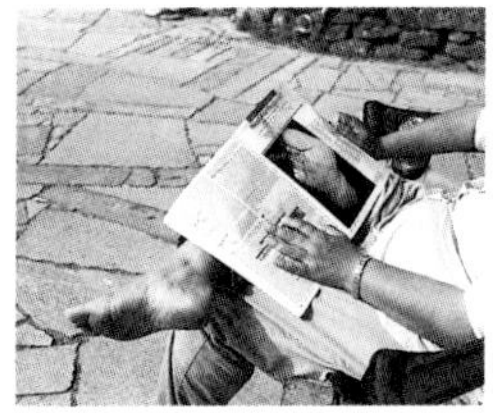

35 Whats your
diagnosis?,
August 2010.

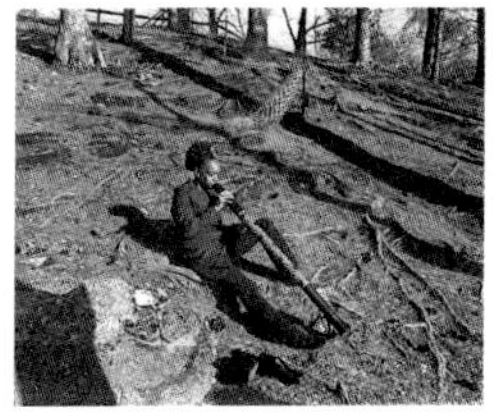

36 Didgeridoo,
May 2011.

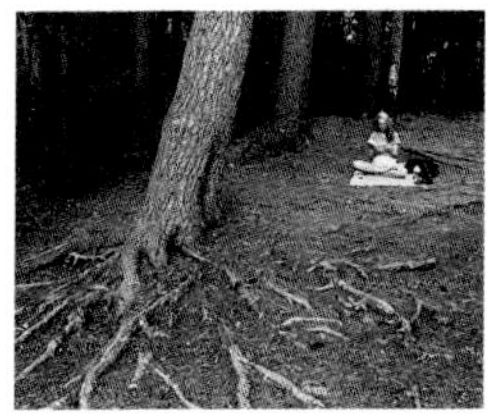

37 Literary pilgrim,
July 2012,

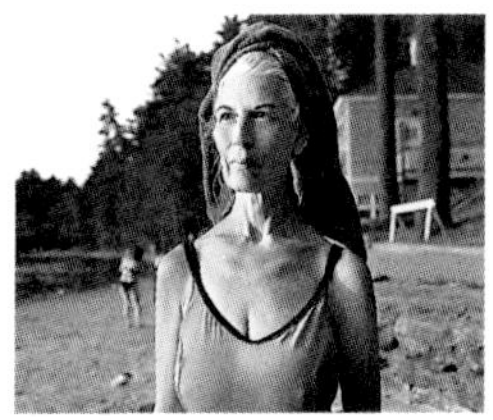

38 Mary,
August 2011.

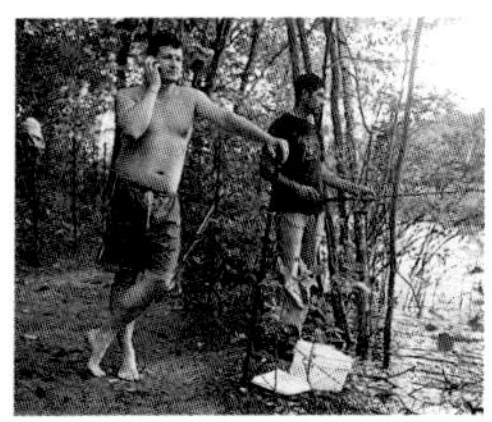

39 Russian parkgoer
on the phone,
July 2010.

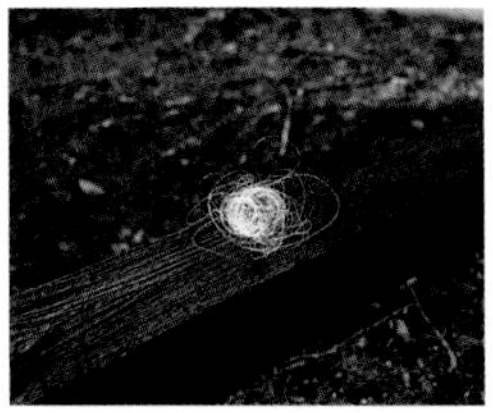

40 Tangled fishing line,
June 2011.

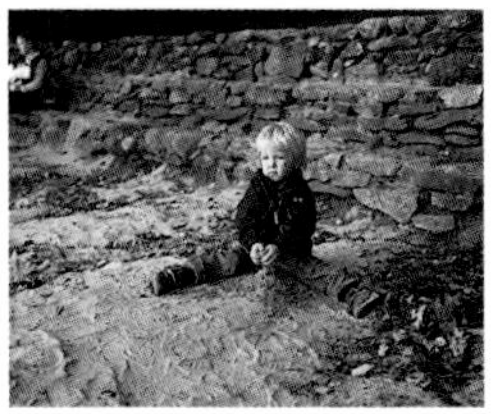

41 Boy, sand through
the fingers,
October 2010.

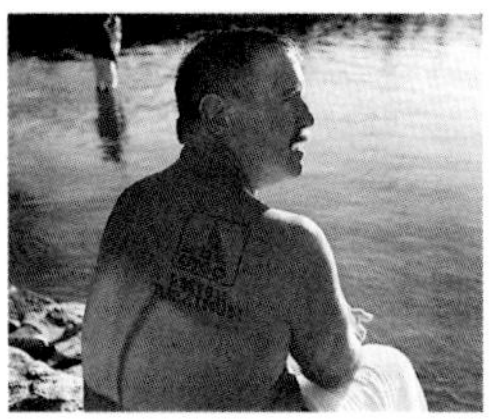

42 One-legged Boston
marathoner with
'Citgo Sign' tattoo,
October 2010.

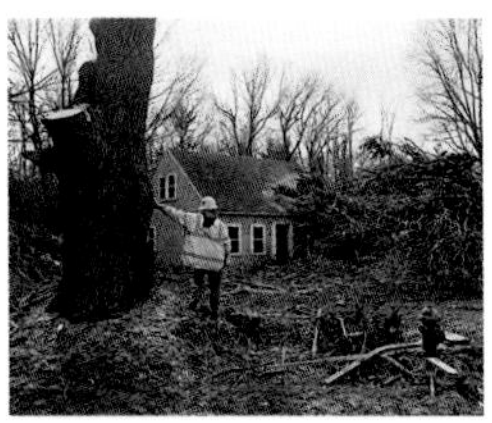

43 Eminent domain, Rt. 2
highway expansion,
March 2013.

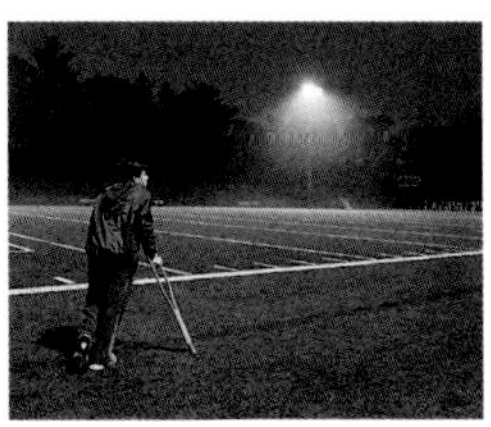

44 High school football
field, Walden Woods,
October 2011.

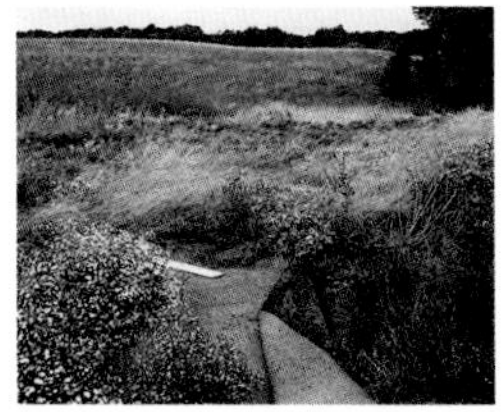

45 Astro turf,
Concord landfill,
October 2011.

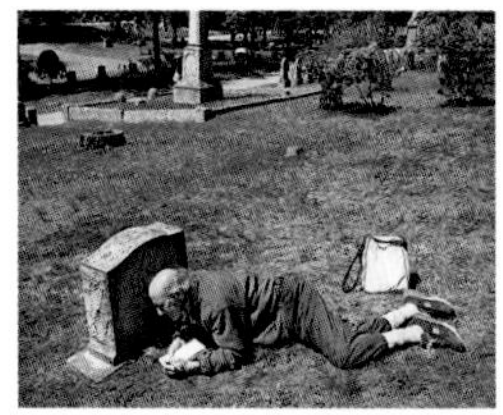

46 Richard Primack;
biologist, and author of
Walden Warming,
recording flowering times,
May 2013.

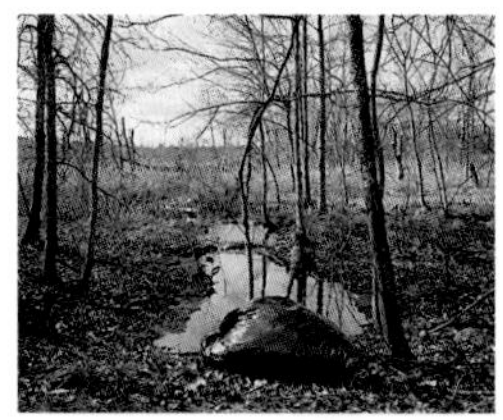

47 Trash near
Baker Bridge,
November 2011.

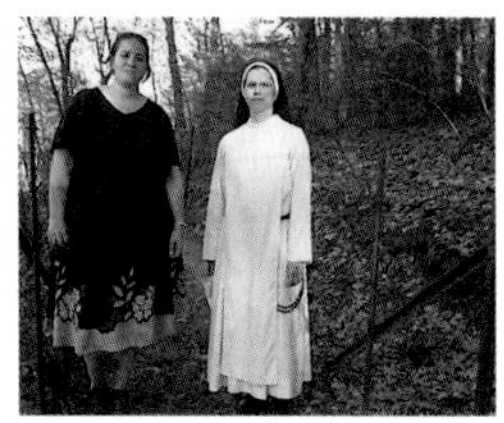

48 A Domenican Sister
of Hawthorne and
friend, May 2013.

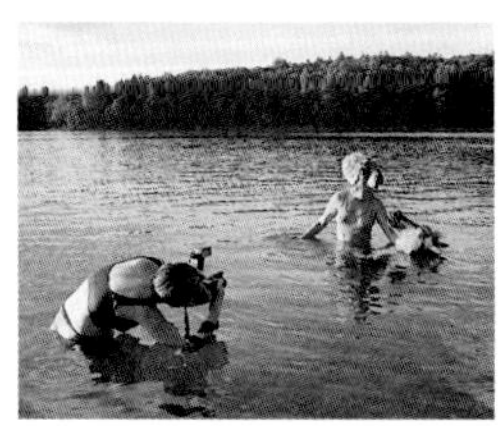

49 Squirrel and Horse,
an artist at work,
August 2013.

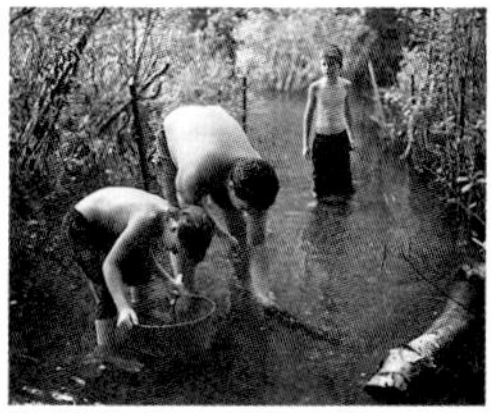

50 Flooded path, high water, fishing, August 2012.

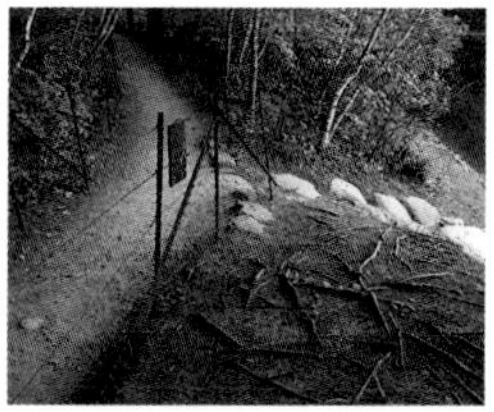

51 Path, erosion, fence, August 2012.

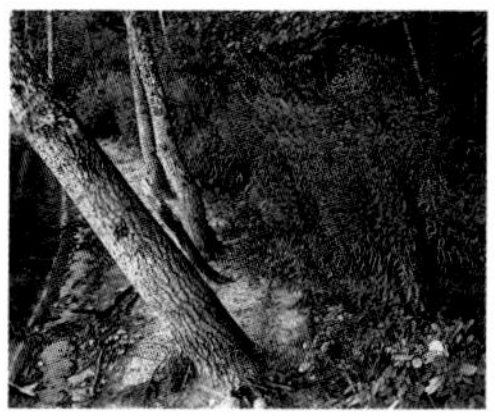

52 Northern shorline, August 2012.

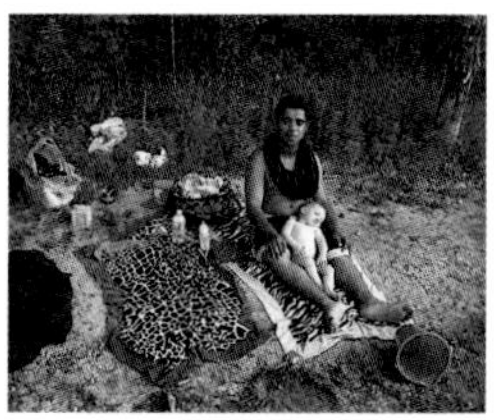

53 Black man, white baby, July 2013.

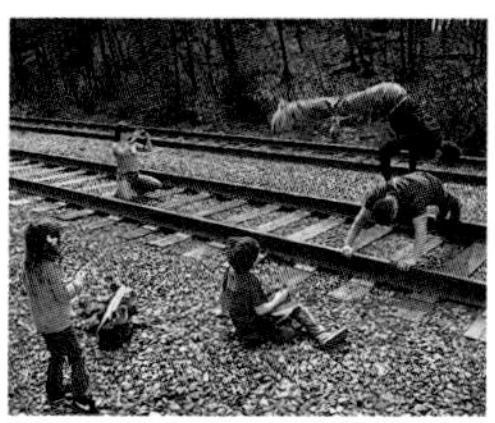

54 A family on Easter, playing on the Fitchburg railroad, April 2013.

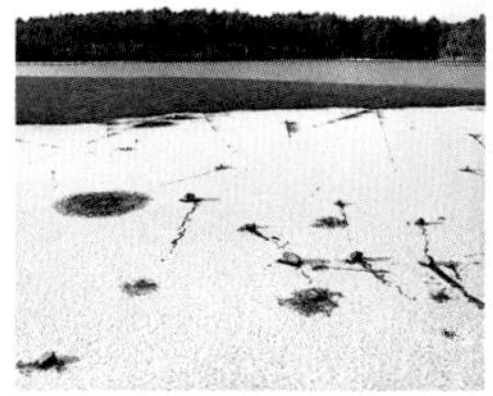

55 Stones cast onto the ice, January 2013.

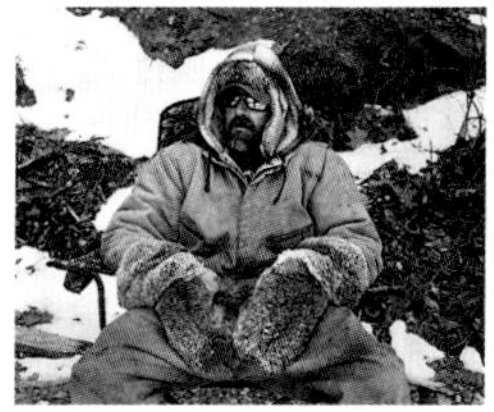

56 Ice fisherman, rabbit fur mitts, January 2011.

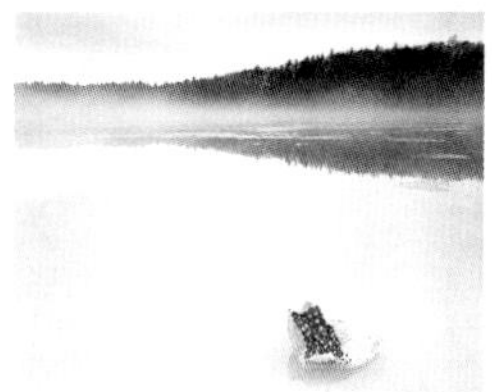

57 Department store plastic bag (Target Corp.), ice melt, March 2011.

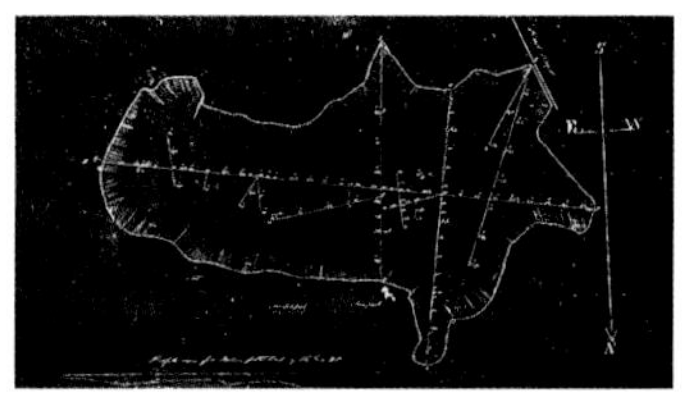

Cover: Henry David Thoreau's Survey of Walden Pond, 1846. *Courtesy Concord Free Public Library.*

Bio

S.B. Walker is an artist living and working in New England. His works have been exhibited internationally and can be found in public and private collections including the *Museum of Fine Arts (Boston)*, the *Fitchburg Art Museum*, the *Smith Museum of Art*, the *David Winton Bell Gallery at Brown University*, the *Maine Museum of Photographic Art,* the *Thoreau Institute*, and the *Prentice and Paul Sack Photographic Trust.*

S.B. Walker is represented by *Janet Borden Inc.*, New York, NY.

Acknowledgments:

I'd like to express my sincere gratitutude to the following individuals and institutions without whose support the vision for this project may not have been fully realized:

Jeff Cramer
The Concord Free Public Library
Lori Foley
John T. Hill
Sven Martson
The Mass Cultural Council
Ernest Morin
Jeanne and Richard S. Press
Richard Reisen
Joel Sternfeld
Alan Trachtenberg
The Vermont Studio Center
The Walden Woods Project

This book is dedicated to Thomas H. Walker.

First edition 2016

Design and sequence by S.B. Walker with consultation from John T. Hill.
This book is set in various weights of Gill Sans and Architype Renner.
Image interpretation by S.B. Walker.

Printed and bound in Germany
ISBN: 978-3-86828-765-3

Kehrer Heidelberg Berlin
www.kehrerverlag.com